Participatory Community Inquiry in the Opioid Epidemic

This book explores a research project focused on finding a community-level response to the opioid epidemic. Grounded in communication ethics, appreciative inquiry, and action research, this book contends that the opioid epidemic in the United States is as much a social disease as it is a pharmaceutical one, arising from a lack of social connection and the "communal literacy" Americans need to deal with the challenges they face together.

Asking how Americans can rediscover their social connection to rebuild vibrant, sustainable communities, the author proposes and tests an approach called Participatory Community Inquiry (PCI), which helps groups acknowledge the social goods that unite them, design practices that protect and promote those goods, and undertake actions that can support their common lives.

Shaping the conversation on how Americans may rediscover and rebuild the community they have lost, this book will be a key resource for researchers, practitioners, and students in communication studies, sociology, and action research interested in social ethics and community development and organizing.

Craig T. Maier is Associate Professor in the Department of Communication & Rhetorical Studies at Duquesne University, USA.

Routledge Focus on Communication Studies

Strategic Communication and Deformative Transparency
Persuasion in Politics, Propaganda, and Public Health
Isaac Nahon-Serfaty

Globalism and Gendering Cancer
Tracking the Trope of Oncogenic Women from the US to Kenya
Miriam O'Kane Mara

Maatian Ethics in a Communication Context
Melba Vélez Ortiz

Enhancing Intercultural Communication in Organizations
Insights From Project Advisers
Edited by Roos Beerkens, Emmanuelle Le Pichon, Roselinde Supheert, Jan D. ten Thije

Communicating Aggression in a Megamedia World
Beata Sierocka

Multigenerational Communication in Organizations
Insights from the Workplace
Michael G. Strawser, Stephanie A. Smith and Bridget Rubenking

Participatory Community Inquiry in the Opioid Epidemic
A New Approach for Communities in Crisis
Craig T. Maier

For more information about this series, please visit: https://www.routledge.com

Participatory Community Inquiry in the Opioid Epidemic

A New Approach for Communities in Crisis

Craig T. Maier

Routledge
Taylor & Francis Group

NEW YORK AND LONDON

First published 2022
by Routledge
605 Third Avenue, New York, NY 10158

and by Routledge
2 Park Square, Milton Park, Abingdon, Oxon, OX14 4RN

Routledge is an imprint of the Taylor & Francis Group, an informa business

Library of Congress Cataloging-in-Publication Data
A catalog record for this title has been requested

ISBN: 9781032152332 (hbk)
ISBN: 9781032153315 (pbk)
ISBN: 9781003243663 (ebk)

DOI: 10.4324/9781003243663

Typeset in Times New Roman
by codeMantra

Contents

Figures

Tables

Acknowledgments

This project required the assistance of a number of people affiliated with the Department of Communication and Rhetorical Studies at Duquesne University in Pittsburgh, Pennsylvania. G. Blake Plavchak and Katherine Rogers formed the core of the research team. Dr. Hannah Karolak, Dr. Emmalee Torisk, and Austin Hestdalen served as facilitators of the inquiry groups. Torisk, Rogers, and Kelly Errera also helped prepare this manuscript for publication. In addition, several students in my Fall 2019 research methods course helped test and refine the framework and provided vital support during the sessions as notetakers and organizers: Anna Bonanno, Chance Broughton, Preston Carmack, Lindsey Laverty, Dominic Lea, Abbey McCann, and Kristen Migliozzi.

Furthermore, I thank Jessica Mann, Angelle Pryor, and Deanna Fracul of Duquesne University's Center for Community-Engaged Teaching and Research, who provided a mini-grant funding crucial logistical support for the inquiry groups.

I am also deeply appreciative of the work of Suzanne Richardson and Tanushree Baijal of Routledge, who were essential in shepherding this project toward publication amidst the stresses and turmoil of the COVID-19 pandemic.

Finally, I am grateful for the support of my wife, Gabriele Maier, and my sons Max and Noah, without whom this project would not have been possible.

Introduction

Rediscovering Each Other in a Time of Crisis

Today, communities across the United States are fighting an epidemic inside of a pandemic in a country without a society. Opioid use disorder continues to be a public health crisis with no clear end in sight. But while many communities have begun to turn the tide, the events of 2020 have revealed alarming deficits in the things these communities need to succeed in their fight: supportive relationships, social trust, institutional stability, economic opportunity, and hope for the future. The institutional response in the United States to the coronavirus outbreak that arose in the early weeks of 2020 was marked by an official death toll that (as of early fall 2021) has eclipsed any other nation on earth, breathtaking institutional incompetence and impotence, an economic collapse unlike anything since the Great Depression, and a frightening willingness to give up at the first sign of difficulty. At the same time, the extraordinary wave of social protest that arose in the wake of the May 25, 2020, murder of George Floyd at the hands of police shed new light on the violence, oppression, inequality, and precarity faced by Americans of color long before but especially during the pandemic, as well as the ways in which American political, legal, economic, social, and educational institutions are not only incapable of responding to these social injustices but are also deeply complicit in them. Although the opioid epidemic, the coronavirus pandemic, and the epidemics of racism and classicism represent different pathologies with fundamentally different etiologies, they all point to fundamental and wholesale failures of American institutional life and leadership.

While these failures have been decades—and, in the case of racial injustice, centuries—in the making, the course to our current crisis was charted in the Reagan-Thatcher revolution of the early 1980s, when policy makers seized upon the mechanism of the free market as the cure for all social ills. "There is no such thing as society," Margaret Thatcher famously told *Woman's Own* (Keay 1987, 30) in the middle

DOI: 10.4324/9781003243663-1

of the decade, advancing an unshakeable faith in what she and countless others took to be the unlimited creative power of lone individuals competing relentlessly in support of their own personal economic self-interest. Pursued with ruthless abandon on both sides of the Atlantic, this individualist vision initiated an economic expansion unlike any other in human history, lifting billions out of poverty worldwide and transforming American society into a gleaming façade of ruthlessly efficient and increasingly unequal consumerism. But as Robert N. Bellah, Richard Madsen, William M. Sullivan, Ann Swidler, and Steven M. Tipton (1991) noted in *The Good Society*, this economic expansion was already corroding every aspect of American civic life. This corrosion continued unabated, and now ordinary Americans must somehow find their way through a risk society unable to cope with the political, social, economic, and environmental hazards that are the cruel side effects of unconstrained economic growth (Beck 1992). But as Ulrich Beck and Elizabeth Beck-Gernsheim (2002) argued, the compulsive individualization of contemporary life leaves people exposed to risk at every level. Although Black and brown people most certainly bear these risks most acutely, many Americans who had considered themselves privileged awakened over the past year to find that they, too, must bear the weight of the world, as Thatcher promised, alone.

The months since the 2020 presidential election in the United States have only slightly ameliorated the situation. By late spring 2021, the election of Joseph Biden to the presidency, a rapid vaccination effort, the prospects of economic recovery, and the conviction of Derek Chauvin for George Floyd's killing all seemed to have walked American society back from the brink. But other signs suggest that Americans still live in vastly different and bitterly divided social worlds. Wild and baseless conspiracy theories about voter fraud in the 2020 election that led to riots at the United States Capitol on January 6, 2021, continue to attract tens of millions of Americans (Edsall 2021; Greenwood 2021). As many as 30 million Americans—a cult that rivals the size of many American religions—adhere to the beliefs of QAnon, which believes, among other things, that the United States government has been infiltrated by Satanic child molesters (Russonello 2021). Widespread institutional mistrust regarding the efficacy and safety of the COVID-19 vaccine has made it all but impossible for the United States to reach the threshold to achieve the herd immunity necessary for a truly safe reopening (Mandavilli 2021). And even though a survey of American adults found that three-quarters agreed with Chauvin's conviction, deep polarization and pessimism on race relations persist along ideological lines (Montanaro 2021). As they uneasily emerge from their pandemic-induced isolation, then, Americans are reentering public life and relearning how to encounter each other at a particularly vulnerable point in their history. They have an opportunity to reset and reshape their lives together. Or they can snap back to the communicative habits, the relational "muscle memory," that got them here in the first place.

This extended study proposes and explores a process of community-level research and intervention called *Participatory Community Inquiry* (PCI) that it hopes will help people rediscover how to engage each other and address the challenges they face together. While the topic is opioid use disorder, this study will not address the problem through the lens of public health, addiction prevention and treatment, or health communication. Rather, it will explore how the opioid epidemic is grounded in the ways Americans have come to interact and, all too often, fail to interact with each other, a concern that speaks to a body of scholarship known as communication ethics. Although it may initially seem at odds with the current emphasis on addiction treatment and harm reduction strategies in responding to substance use disorder (see Boden 2018; Carroll, Green, and Noonan 2018; Department of Health and Human Services 2018; Hulsey et al. 2019; Kolla and Strike 2019), this approach reflects a growing body of research suggesting that the opioid crisis grows out of deep dysfunctions in American communities that require urgent attention (McLean 2016; Zoorob and Salemi 2017; Becker 2018; Klinenberg 2018; Saloner et al. 2018; Case and Deaton 2020). In this sense, this study contends that we should not be surprised that a country with a raging opioid epidemic is also a country that, despite its profound wealth, cannot respond successfully to the coronavirus pandemic, persistent racial and economic inequality, or any other challenge that other nations lacking this impressive material endowment seem to handle with comparative ease. Simply put, the United States is vulnerable because its people have forgotten how to build community together, a capacity this study calls *communal literacy*. PCI, as a form of community intervention and education, strives to build that capacity and sustain it.

Drawing from the fields of appreciative inquiry, communication studies, and action research, this extended research report explores PCI by reporting on a pilot study on community-level responses to the opioid epidemic undertaken in the fall of 2019 in a neighborhood of Pittsburgh, Pennsylvania, that will be called "Southton."[1] Chapter 1 frames the study by talking about the opioid epidemic as a crisis of social connection, with a special focus on the neighborhood where the research took place. Then, Chapter 2 shows how Ronald C. Arnett,

Janie M. Harden Fritz, and Leanne M. Bell McManus's (2018) work on communication ethics literacy lays the foundation for communal literacy, a broad capacity that supports community life by helping persons attend to what matters around them, be present to each other, and care for what they share in common. Chapter 3 outlines PCI as an approach that fosters communal literacy that (1) operates with an appreciative intent focused on defining the social goods that draw community members together, (2) proposes and tests communicative practices of community building that help community members live out those goods, and (3) designs actions that strengthen the community's capacity to care for its common life. After summarizing the study's methodology in Chapter 4 and reporting the results in Chapter 5, Chapter 6 will reflect on the tentative findings, discuss the study's limitations, and consider ways PCI can be scaled and strengthened. To be sure, this pilot project is only a single effort in a particular place, so we should be cautious about generalizing its findings. But as an experiment, it may help shape the conversation on how Americans may rediscover and rebuild the society they have lost.

Obviously, this study hopes to participate in the conversation surrounding possible responses to opioid use disorder in the United States. But because it emerges from the field of communication ethics, PCI has the potential to reach beyond the opioid epidemic to offer a flexible approach that can help communities not only in the United States but also around the world begin to respond to a variety of issues and concerns. Making this move means this study can also contribute both to the study of communication ethics and the practice of community development and leadership. The field of communication ethics is, by its very nature, highly philosophical and theoretical. This abstraction can create misunderstandings as to the purpose and value of ethical reflection on communication and, in turn, make it difficult to see how communication ethics can foster the types of community-level and institutional interventions so urgently needed in contemporary society. As Deborah Eicher-Catt (2013) writes, communication ethics is often mistakenly viewed, even by some who write on the topic, as merely a matter of conversational etiquette or social hygiene that promotes consensus and conformity at the expense of difficult conversations or, even worse, insulates privileged audiences from having to hear or respond to uncomfortable truths. Eicher-Catt rejects this line of argument, emphasizing that communication ethics must be understood as a field that strives to offer people and communities ways of negotiating even the deepest of differences. In this way, PCI offers a compelling approach that connects the theoretical richness of communication ethics scholarship to the practice of community life.

Walking communication ethics into practice in this way can help this study contribute to community leadership, organizing, and capacity building, as well. Communities today are beset by what Zaid Hassan (2014) calls *complex challenges* involving economic and social inequality, police violence, environmental risks, and countless other issues that are so multidimensional and shapeless that they are impossible to define, let alone address in any conclusive way. As they break into the public sphere, these difficulties create a particularly "wicked" form of chronic crisis that destroys everything it touches (Maier and Crist 2017). While activist groups are vital in raising the alarm about these challenges, and while the crises that emerge from them are vital cries for social justice, meeting these concerns requires a sustained form of community engagement that brings a diverse array of perspectives, interests, and stakeholders to the table. But as John Gastil and William M. Keith (2005) observed 15 years ago, Americans have increasingly been unable to have these types of difficult conversations, preferring instead to remain locked in bubbles of ideological purity that make it impossible to discuss *anything*, let alone anything of importance. PCI offers a framework that can help communities build the capacity for these conversations to occur, allowing Americans to rediscover each other in a time of crisis. The coming decade of extraordinary—indeed, existential—social, political, economic, and environmental uncertainty makes the recovery of American community life and the social benefits it brings more urgent than ever.

Note

1   "Southton" is a pseudonym.

References

Arnett, Ronald C., Janie M. Harden Fritz, and Leeanne M. Bell McManus. 2018. *Communication Ethics Literacy: Dialogue and Difference*. 2nd ed. Dubuque, IA: Kendall Hunt Publishing.

Beck, Ulrich. 1992. *Risk Society: Towards a New Modernity*. Translated by Mark Ritter. Thousand Oaks, CA: Sage.

Beck, Ulrich, and Elisabeth Beck-Gernsheim. 2002. *Individualization: Institutionalized Individualism and Its Social and Political Causes*. Thousand Oaks, CA: Sage.

Becker, Daniel M. 2018. "The Addicts on Main Street." *The Journal of Law, Medicine & Ethics* 46, no. 3: 610–14. https://doi.org/10.1177/1073110518804211.

Bellah, Robert N., Richard Madsen, William M. Sullivan, Ann Swidler, and Steven M. Tipton. 1991. *The Good Society.* New York: Vintage.

Boden, Sarah. 2018. "Carrick Could Be Site of City's Newest Needle Exchange." *WESA-FM*, September 13, 2018. https://www.wesa.fm/post/carrick-could-be-site-citys-newest-needle-exchange#stream/0.

Carroll, Jennifer J., Traci C. Green, and Rita K. Noonan. 2018. *Evidence-Based Strategies for Preventing Opioid Overdose: What's Working in the United States.* Atlanta: Centers for Disease Control and Prevention. https://www.cdc.gov/drugoverdose/pdf/pubs/2018-evidence-based-strategies.pdf.

Case, Anne, and Angus Deaton. 2020. *Deaths of Despair and the Future of Capitalism.* Princeton, NJ: Princeton University Press.

Department of Health and Human Services. 2018. *Naloxone: The Opioid Reversal Drug That Saves Lives.* Washington, DC: Department of Health and Human Services. https://www.hhs.gov/opioids/sites/default/files/2018-12/naloxone-coprescribing-guidance.pdf.

Edsall, Thomas B. 2021. "The QAnon Delusion Has Not Loosened Its Grip." *The New York Times*, February 3, 2021. https://www.nytimes.com/2021/02/03/opinion/qanon-conspiracy-theories.html/.

Eicher-Catt, Deborah. 2013. "A Semiotic Interpretation of Authentic Civility: Preserving the Ineffable for the Good of the Common." *Communication Quarterly* 61, no. 1: 1–17. https://doi.org/10.1080/01463373.2012.718727.

Gastil, John, and William M. Keith. 2005. "A Nation That (Sometimes) Likes to Talk: A Brief History of Public Deliberation in the United States." In *The Deliberative Democracy Handbook*, edited by John Gastil and Peter Levine, 3–19. San Francisco, CA: Jossey-Bass.

Greenwood, Max. 2021. "53 Percent of Republicans Say Trump Is True President: Poll." *The Hill*, May 25, 2021. https://thehill.com/homenews/campaign/555256-53-percent-of-republicans-say-trump-is-true-president-poll/.

Hassan, Zaid. 2014. *The Social Labs Revolution: A New Approach to Solving Our Most Complex Challenges.* San Francisco, CA: Berrett-Koehler Publishers.

Hulsey, Eric, Fizza Shah, Peter Jhon, LaToya Warren, and Erin Dalton. 2019. *Data Brief: Naloxone Distribution in the Allegheny County Jail to Prevent Overdose.* Pittsburgh, PA: Allegheny County Department of Human Services, Allegheny County Health Department and Allegheny County Jail. https://www.alleghenycountyanalytics.us/wp-content/uploads/2019/02/18-ACDHS-27-NaloxoneACJ-022119_v2.pdf.

Keay, Douglas. 1987. "Interview with Margaret Thatcher." *Woman's Own*, September 23, 1987. Klinenberg, Eric. 2018. *Palaces for the People: How Social Infrastructure Can Help Fight Inequality, Polarization, and the Decline of Civic Life.* New York: Crown.

Kolla, Gillian, and Carol Strike. 2019. "'It's Too Much, I'm Getting Really Tired of It': Overdose Response and Structural Vulnerabilities among Harm Reduction Workers in Community Settings." *International Journal of Drug Policy* 74: 127–35. https://doi.org/10.1016/j.drugpo.2019.09.012.

Maier, Craig T., and Jonathan R. Crist. 2017. "From 'Wicked Crisis' to Responsive Witness: Jean-Luc Marion and the American Roman Catholic Sexual-Abuse Scandal." *Southern Communication Journal* 82, no. 3: 164–74. https://doi.org/10.1080/1041794x.2017.1315453.

Mandavilli, Apoorva. 2021. "Reaching 'Herd Immunity' Is Unlikely in the U.S., Experts Now Believe." *The New York Times*, May 3, 2021. https://www.nytimes.com/2021/05/03/health/covid-herd-immunity-vaccine.html.

McLean, Katherine. 2016. "There's Nothing Here": Deindustrialization as Risk Environment for Overdose. *International Journal of Drug Policy* 29: 19–26. https://doi.org/10.1016/j.drugpo.2016.01.009.

Montanaro, Dominico. 2021. "Where Views on Race and Police Stand a Year after George Floyd's Murder." *NPR*, May 17, 2021. https://www.npr.org/2021/05/17/996857103/poll-details-the-very-different-views-of-black-and-white-americans-on-race-and-p.

Russonello, Giovanni. 2021. "QAnon Now as Popular in U.S. as Some Major Religions, Poll Suggests." *The New York Times*, May 27, 2021. https://www.nytimes.com/2021/05/27/us/politics/qanon-republicans-trump.html?searchResultPosition=1/.

Saloner, Brendan, Emma E. McGinty, Leo Beletsky, Ricky Bluthenthal, Chris Beyrer, Michael Botticelli, and Susan G. Sherman. 2018. "A Public Health Strategy for the Opioid Crisis." *Public Health Reports* 133, no. 1: 24S–34S. https://doi.org/10.1177/0033354918793627.

Zoorob, Michael J., and Jason L. Salemi. 2017. "Bowling Alone, Dying Together: The Role of Social Capital in Mitigating the Drug Overdose Epidemic in the United States." *Drug and Alcohol Dependence* 173: 1–9. https://doi.org/10.1016/j.drugalcdep.2016.12.011.

1   Opioid Use Disorder

A Social Fabric Come Undone

In his book *Dreamland*, Sam Quinones (2015) depicts the opioid epidemic as a national catastrophe emerging at the confluence of a number of factors: the increasing awareness among physicians of the importance of treating chronic pain, a widespread but profoundly mistaken belief that opioids taken to treat such pain would be non-addictive, reluctance of health insurance companies to invest in non-pharmaceutical pain treatments, the collapse of Rust Belt economies leaving hundreds of thousands of Americans unemployed and in physical and psychological distress, physicians and pharmaceutical companies eager to profit from supplying drugs such as Oxy-Contin to these people, and illegal drug cartels more than willing to fill any gaps in that supply with heroin and fentanyl. As Anne Case and Angus Deaton (2020) observe, all of these trends intensified in the years following the Great Recession. According to the National Institute on Drug Abuse (2021), deaths from opioid overdoses in the United States rose from 18,515 in 2007 to 47,600 in 2017, a number greater than the number of combat deaths in the Vietnam War. In 2018, the number of deaths nationwide was only slightly lower at 46,802, making opioid use once again the most common cause of overdose death in the United States. In 2019, the most recent year that statistics are available, the number skyrocketed to an all-time high of 49,860 deaths. And although the official toll for 2020 is unlikely to be known for some time, early statistics show that the emotional, social, and economic stresses of COVID-19, combined with stay-at-home orders, could very well push overdose deaths even higher (Baumgartner and Radley 2021; Mason et al. 2021).

This chapter explores the struggles of the neighborhood of Southton, one of a cluster of four neighborhoods in a single Pittsburgh City Council district highlighted as the center of the city's opioid overdoses and deaths. Drawing on research connecting opioid use disorder to

DOI: 10.4324/9781003243663-2

deeper social and relational dynamics within American life, this chapter seeks to situate opioid use disorder within a broader context of community decline. Certainly, this discussion does not discount the hard work of public health professionals, treatment centers, and others in helping people recovering from this devastating disease. But if the opioid epidemic is a social illness as much as it is a pharmaceutical one, then its treatment requires attention to social factors, as well. What is more, locating the roots of opioid use disorder within the fraying social fabric of American life reminds us that the opioid epidemic is connected to a much deeper affliction demanding a much more radical response.

The Struggles of Southton

Despite the challenges they have faced, Southton and its surrounding neighborhoods have been making steady progress in reducing the opioid epidemic's lethality. In Allegheny County, where Pittsburgh is located, policy makers and treatment providers focused their resources at the height of the crisis on medication-assisted treatment (Allegheny County Department of Human Services et al. 2017), as well as on harm reduction interventions such as targeted naloxone distribution (Hulsey et al. 2019; Kolla and Strike 2019) and syringe services programs (Boden 2018) that can make using opioids safer. These strategies align with guidance at the national level from both the Centers for Disease Control and Prevention (Carroll, Green, and Noonan 2018) and the Department of Health and Human Services (2018), which prescribe collaborative approaches blending naloxone distribution, needle exchanges, and medication-assisted treatment in jails, emergency rooms, and community settings, as well as increased outreach to health care providers to reduce the prescription of opioids in pain management, Good Samaritan laws releasing bystanders from any legal liability arising from helping persons who have overdosed, and the inclusion of fentanyl in routine drug screens. These efforts bore fruit: As the number of fatal overdoses nationally increased from 2017 to 2019 (National Institute on Drug Abuse 2020), statistics from the Pennsylvania Department of Health (2020) show that the number of opioid overdose deaths in the Commonwealth between 2017 and 2019 *decreased* from 5,398 to an estimated 4,125, a 23.6 percent decline. The mortality rate in Allegheny County decreased slightly faster, dropping 27 percent over the same period, from 981 deaths in 2017 to 716 deaths in 2019 (Overdose Free PA n.d.), the year during which the current study took place.

Yet, these intervention strategies, important as they are, only manage what Katherine McLean (2016), following the work of Tim Rhodes (2009), calls the *micro-level risk environments* that

> concern the physical spaces of drug use, local norms around drug consumption and strategies for its policing, lack of income and access to health care, and the effective (un)availability of harm reduction programs, educational materials or tools (including clean syringes and naloxone).
>
> (22–23)

Writing about the experiences of people struggling with opioid use disorder in McKeesport, a city in Allegheny County only about a 30-minute drive away from Southton, McLean (2016, 24) emphasizes the importance of the *macro-level risk environment*—"the stagnant economy, institutional culture, and overall atmosphere" that interacts with, complicates, and frustrates micro-level interventions. McLean's (2016, 24) subjects "were overwhelmingly pessimistic about the feasibility and success of any overdose interventions that did not simultaneously address the stifling poverty of the region or the alienation and despair of McKeesport's dwindling populace." Although naloxone clearly saves lives, McLean (2016, 24) concludes that addressing opioid use disorder requires paying attention to what is lacking in the macro-level environment, which includes "not only jobs but also residents, effective government, social events and activities" that give people constructive alternatives to drugs. McLean's study suggests that understanding the macro-level risk environment can not only shed light on the deeper, structural factors that lead people to become addicted to drugs but also help plan interventions aimed at the root causes of opioid use disorder, which is increasingly understood to reflect social, political, and economic causes as much as individual differences and choices (Becker 2018; Saloner et al. 2018).

Understanding this broader context may explain why the epidemic has been so pronounced in Southton. In comparison to Pittsburgh as a whole, Southton is primarily white: According to the 2018 American Community Survey, 89.7 percent of its 13,884 residents are white and only 4.6 percent are Black, whereas 66.9 percent of Pittsburgh's 303,587 population is white and 23.2 percent Black. Southton is also wealthier: The median income is $54,746, in contrast to the city of Pittsburgh's median income of $47,417, and 71.3 percent of households own their own homes, while only 46.9 percent of the homes in Pittsburgh are owner-occupied. Still, the neighborhood, much like many parts of Pittsburgh itself, has struggled since the demise of the steel industry in southwestern Pennsylvania during the mid-1980s, a collapse journalist John Hoerr (1988) frames as a massive trauma event touching every aspect of the region's life and people. The loss of stable employment forever shattered a social contract that until then had presupposed perpetual prosperity. After decades of fighting bitter and at times bloody struggles for dominance, Hoerr writes, labor and management had forged a tacit and brutally simple compromise: Management would pay high wages in return for unions refusing to strike. Mill towns resisted anything that would alter the tense detente, giving rise to what Hoerr sees as a mentality defined by low expectations and an even narrower capacity to adapt to change. When foreign competition and economic pressures made the social contract null and void, the effects were profound. Though the workers attempted to remain resilient in the face of change, their neighborhoods quickly died, young people left as soon as they could, suicide rates increased, fragmented local municipalities went bankrupt, and the public infrastructure fell into decay.

Some parts of the city have rebounded since then, driven by the health care, higher education, financial services, and technology sectors. But neighborhoods have not benefited equally. In some areas, the unevenness in development surely comes down to structural racism, but in places such as Southton, separated from the city center and the university communities by the Monongahela River, the cause may be more geographic. But regardless of the reason, Southton, like the other neighborhoods in its city council district, has been left behind. Southton Boulevard, which cuts through the community and was once a thriving business district, is a shadow of its former self, defined by cell phone stores, pizza parlors, and litter. And while not technically a food desert—Southton has a few convenience stores and smaller markets where residents can buy some necessities, and public transit is decent—the neighborhood of nearly 14,000 people has only one real supermarket located on its edge. Participants in the study reported having to travel outside of the community for much of their shopping, leading to a sense of dependency, frustration, and decline.

Although the decline of Southton Boulevard and the lack of quality shopping may seem to be merely cosmetic, Eric Klinenberg (2018) contends that these spaces have tremendous implications for the quality of the social connections that people make. When people work together, shop together, encounter each other, and feel safe together, they have the opportunity to sustain relationships that provide vital resources to help them thrive in normal times and survive moments of crisis.

"Local, face-to-face interactions—at the school, the playground, and the corner diner—are the building blocks of all public life," Klinenberg (2018, 5) writes, and without these interactions, social trust declines, participation in institutional life suffers, and people experience higher levels of alienation that harm their physical and emotional health. The results of this social decline increasingly emerge in the opioid epidemic in what Princeton University economists Anne Case and Angus Deaton (2020) have provocatively called "deaths of despair."

Social Despair, Social Connection, and Social Capital

To be sure, Case and Deaton's (2020) work needs to be treated with care. Even as their catchphrase has captured the imaginations of pundits and policy makers alike, numerous researchers have raised important concerns. Alleviating "despair" is an ambiguous basis for public policy, they have argued, and the focus on the experiences of non-Hispanic whites without college degrees ignores the despair endemic to Black, Latinx, and Native American communities for centuries (Diez Roux 2017; Komro 2018; Muennig et al. 2018). Yet, Case and Deaton are not so much writing marginalized communities out of the story in favor of working-class whites as they are making a sobering commentary on the widespread dysfunction, vulnerability, and inequality now tearing at the fabric of *every* aspect of American life. Today, large segments of Americans, regardless of race, now find themselves leading isolated, unvalued, and precarious lives in a country that has left them behind. They argue that as these disparities widen and become more apparent to those on the bottom, and as those on the top move more aggressively to protect themselves from a similar fate, the despair and anger will only deepen, with devastating social consequences for decades to come.

Richard Sennett (1998) writes that the profound despair Case and Deaton (2020) see as being experienced by ever-larger and ever-more diverse percentages of American society suggests a powerful story that helps disenfranchised people make sense of their experience. But the story of despair, with its combination of self-blame and frustration at one's own circumstances and anger at the elites believed to be responsible for creating those conditions, is profoundly corrosive for community life. Lilly Shanahan et al. (2019) observe that despair, as a construct, speaks to a complex web of cognitive factors (e.g., thoughts of worthlessness or hopelessness), emotional factors (e.g., feelings of sadness, anger, or frustration), behavioral factors (e.g., reckless or self-destructive actions), and biological factors (e.g., experiences of exhaustion, dysregulation, or depletion). Social as well as individual despair can spread like a virus throughout entire communities and relational networks, and Shanahan and her colleagues argue that it can lead to lethal results in the form of suicidal ideation and alcohol and substance use disorders. Furthermore, such despair is spreading: Americans in all categories have reported diminishing levels of happiness and social trust, and they have been increasingly likely to see their standard of living as declining and unfair, with far-reaching implications for how they interact with others (Muennig et al. 2018).

How people engage each other can be more important to opioid use disorder than we may initially think. In many ways, Thomas de Quincey's (1995) account of his experiences of opioid use two centuries ago, which begins with the death of his father, failure at school, and a period of homelessness and near-starvation on the streets of London, may reflect the rule rather than the exception. Increasing research suggests that an area's overall relational climate, like economic factors that Case and Deaton (2020) discuss, is part of the macro-level risk environment that creates the conditions for opioids to take hold (McLean 2016; Becker 2018). Recent neurological studies by Tristen K. Inagaki, Laura I. Hazlett, and Carmen Andreescu (2019, 2020), for instance, have described how opioids can simulate feelings of social warmth and connection in the brain, suggesting that users of opioids may be compensating for the absence of caring relationships around them. This finding may give some insight into why the social rejection and stigmatization that people with opioid use disorder experience complicate their recovery (Komro 2018; Tsai et al. 2019). It also illuminates the role that the weak work, familial, and religious ties of working-class men—and the "haphazard lives" that this lack of deep attachment may encourage these men to lead—might play in their high rate of suicide and drug overdose (Edin et al. 2019, 221). Opioids, prescribed to numb deep physical pain, prove to be equally effective as a self-prescription for the pain of social dislocation and absence.

The concern over the role of social attachment in shaping the macro-level risk environment also points to Robert Putnam's (2000) foundational work on *social capital*. In his discussion, Putnam cites the research of several others, including L. J. Hanifan, whom he credits for coining the term, as well as Jane Jacobs, Glenn Loury, Pierre Bourdieu, Ekkehart Schlicht, and James S. Colman, but Putnam's formulation is important for this project because of its clarity, ease of operationalization, and direct connection to the problems of community life in the United States. For Putnam, "social capital refers to connections among individuals—social networks and the norms of reciprocity and trustworthiness that arise from them" (2000, 19). Like *economic capital*, which allows people to work and gives people the ability to support and provide for themselves and their families; *physical capital*, which speaks to their access to the basic goods they need to lead a dignified life; and *cultural capital*, which reflects the skills and information they need to make decisions and respond to the world, social capital speaks to the bonds of reciprocity and trust that draw people together, allow them to exchange one form of capital for another, and, in turn, maintain and even increase their quality of life.

Because it does not show up directly in people's bank accounts, driveways, or curriculum vitae, social capital is easy to ignore. But Putnam (2000) emphasizes that this invisible resource may actually be the key to all of the others. It comes in two forms that perform different but equally important roles. *Bonding* social capital, Putnam argues, strengthens the ties within a particular group of people, as when a group of immigrants pools their resources to create a home for themselves in a new place, a marginalized community joins together to mobilize and protest conditions that are afflicting them, a young person consults an aunt or uncle about pursuing a career as a welder, or parents ask a friend for help getting their child with special needs into a better preschool. In each of these situations, bonding capital looks inward, allowing people within the same social space to support each other. As a result, it can be extraordinarily important when it comes to opioid use disorder. Indeed, William Cloud and Robert Granfield (2008) underscore the importance of this sense of belonging in developing the "recovery capital" necessary to succeed in treatment.

Yet, bonding social capital alone is insufficient for community cohesion and, if left to its own devices, can actually be harmful. Putnam (2000, 350) notes that bonding has a "dark side," in that it can easily become exclusive and exclusionary, locking some people out as it links others together. For this reason, Putnam argues that *bridging* social capital is essential in providing an essential counterbalance. Looking outward instead of inward, it connects bonded groups together and permits them to share information, help others, and care for social goods across lines of difference. Such connections might help the immigrant group described above broaden their webs of social support, the marginalized community find friends in higher places, the young person answer vocational questions beyond the knowledge of their relatives, and the parents expand the scope of the educational possibilities for their child. When both types of social capital are strong within a community, Putnam contends, the exchanges that occur within and between social networks are essential in helping people find work, learn how best to use the limited goods at their disposal, and get the information they need to make sense out of a complex world. Going farther, Klinenberg (2018) observes that strong social capital can even save lives in moments of crisis because it allows people to coordinate complex actions and care for each other.

Nevertheless, Putnam (2000) contends that declining participation in virtually every type of voluntary association in the United States, from churches and trade unions to rotary clubs and amateur bowling leagues, has taken a toll on social capital, with damaging consequences not only for Americans' economic and political lives but also in their physical and emotional health. Indeed, Michael J. Zoorob and Jason L. Salemi's (2017) comparison of county-level data on social capital and opioid mortality finds that levels of social capital correlate negatively with overdose deaths. For Zoorob and Salemi, the intensity of the opioid epidemic in a particular area depends on the strength, complexity, and diversity of residents' relational networks, their level of community involvement, their sense of feeling "at home" in their neighborhood, their ability to get along with others, and their ability to trust people, especially those in positions of authority. In a study of a rural area deeply affected by opioids, Vicki Simpson (2020) makes a similar argument, contending that a community's ability to resist opioid use disorder depends in large part on its social capital: whether or not it is a thriving place where people want to stay and live, a welcoming place where opioid use disorder is not stigmatized, a caring place open to families and children, and a trusting place where residents have faith both in the police and educational institutions. This research opens the possibility that social capital may be a two-way indicator for communities struggling with opioid use. Looking in one direction, deficiencies in social capital can be seen as a sign of possible risk. But in the other direction, strengthening social capital may serve as a means of intervention that can help communities negotiate deficiencies in other areas.

An earlier study conducted in Southton and the surrounding communities in the fall of 2017 (Maier 2018) suggests that these dynamics were in play in the area where the current study took place. Grounded in appreciative inquiry, the 2017 study interviewed 20 public safety and public health professionals tasked with leading the community's response to the opioid epidemic, with the intent of locating strengths and opportunities in meeting the challenges the neighborhoods faced, as well as defining aspirations that could guide the community forward and concrete results that could help establish meaningful goals. Throughout the interviews, however, a curious pattern emerged.

When interviewed about their perceptions of the communities' strengths and opportunities in meeting the epidemic and asked to imagine what these communities might look like if they could meet the challenge effectively, those closest to the epidemic responded much differently than those farther away. When prompted to consider the communities' strengths, four professionals who could be considered first responders said they could not think of any strengths or opportunities for the community at all. And when invited to discuss their hopes and visions for a post-epidemic vision, five participants—three of whom also found it impossible to see any strengths—struggled because they had given up on the future altogether. "There was no middle ground," the study found. "Participants either believed that the community could respond successfully or rejected any such hopes as naïve" (Maier 2018, 65). The disparity in the answers is remarkable, but *what* they said is not as important as *where* they said it. The closer a participant was geographically to the affected communities—that is, whether they were walking the streets of Southton as opposed to sitting in an air-conditioned university or city government office across the river—the higher the despair.

The sense of hopelessness and helplessness in this previous study was all the more striking and unexpected because it came from professionals whose role and training should have offered them a greater sense of agency and resilience. But they felt this way not only because of the scale of the problem they faced but also because they felt abandoned in the face of what they felt was an impossible job. One participant reported feeling that "'we're pretty much left on our own to deal with the problem,'" while another "expressed frustration with those who, as one participant put it, 'sit in their own ivory tower' while ignoring the life-and-death reality on the ground" (Maier 2018, 65). The stresses of dealing with the epidemic, along with a lack of control and support, had left them cynical, disengaged, and traumatized by their work. Their responses pointed to even deeper community-level challenges, particularly a culture of stigmatization and relational toxicity captured on bumper stickers urging people to "Shoot Your Local Heroin Dealer." One interviewee, for example, reported intervening to help an overdose patient who had been so humiliated by their doctors and nurses that they left the hospital immediately with nothing but a box of Naloxone and a business card.

The toxicity translated to encounters with authorities, as well. Perhaps reflecting the history of contentious labor-management relations Hoerr (1988) describes, relationships between residents and outside authorities can be complicated in the community where the current study took place. While the current study was being developed, for instance, a routine community meeting in a neighborhood adjacent to Southton nearly erupted into violence when a group of protesters rose up against a local substance use disorder treatment agency's plan to put a needle exchange van on one of its streets. From the perspective of the agency and local government representatives, the protest seemed to be an irrational response of an intransigent minority ignorant of the best practices of addiction medicine. But the protestors, as aggressive as they were, had a point: Residents had spent years trying to remove a drug dealer who lived on the very street where the agency wanted to park its van, and the prospect of a needle exchange so close by not only triggered residents' traumatic memories but also seemed to promise that their pain would return. The street needed sidewalks, the protesters argued, not needle exchanges. The fact that the treatment agency could not help them address this need—building sidewalks, after all, was completely outside of its mission—underscored the broken relationship.

Stories like these suggest that Southton is a community where social networks, especially those that bridge between groups, are not particularly strong, social engagement is low, and relational toxicity between both peers and people of differing levels of authority is high. In other words, the neighborhood is struggling with a deficit of social capital. And today, despite the hard-won progress the community has made in response to the opioid epidemic, the coronavirus pandemic is poised to exploit the vulnerabilities low social capital brings. Although it is too early to draw any definitive conclusions about the relationship between COVID-19 and opioid use, people with opioid use disorder are particularly at risk from the pandemic because of the effects of opioids on the respiratory system and of the secondary effects of substance use, including homelessness and incarceration, that can put people into close proximity with each other (National Institute on Drug Abuse 2020). At the same time, measures taken to contain the virus's spread can inhibit access to medication and treatment, increasing the likelihood of overdoses and overdose deaths (Becker and Fiellin 2020).

But just as important, the coronavirus threatens to damage an already weakened social fabric. Social distancing, however necessary it may be, is fundamentally altering how people relate to each other for the foreseeable future. The need to keep six feet apart from others outside of one's "bubble"; the impossibility of handshakes, hugs, and other forms of consensual social touching that ordinarily provide comfort; the inability to see others' faces when talking with them; the continuing confusion and conflict around wearing masks; the closures of public spaces like churches, libraries, and schools where people would normally gather, connect, and grow; and the disruption of employment prospects, especially for young people—all these things accentuate the despair and social alienation at the core of the opioid epidemic and raise the possibility for a resurgence of opioid use disorder in the years to come. As a result, now more than ever, combating opioid use disorder also means looking for ways of reweaving the social fabric itself. Yet, as the next chapter suggests, this task is extraordinarily complex.

References

Allegheny County Department of Human Services, Allegheny County Health Department, Community Care Behavioral Health Organization, and Allegheny HealthChoices, Inc. 2017. *Joint Position Statement on Medication-Assisted Treatment for Opioid Use Disorders in Allegheny County.* Pittsburgh, PA: Allegheny County Department of Human Services, Allegheny County Health Department, Community Care Behavioral Health Organization, and Allegheny HealthChoices, Inc. https://www.alleghenycountyanalytics.us/wp-content/uploads/2017/01/MAT-Position-Paper.pdf.

Baumgartner, Jesse C., and David C. Radley. 2021. "The Spike in Drug Overdose Deaths during the COVID-19 Pandemic and Policy Options to Move Forward." *The Commonwealth Fund*, March 25, 2021. https://www.commonwealthfund.org/blog/2021/spike-drug-overdose-deaths-during-covid-19-pandemic-and-policy-options-move-forward.

Becker, Daniel M. 2018. "The Addicts on Main Street." *The Journal of Law, Medicine & Ethics* 46, no. 3: 610–14. https://doi.org/10.1177/1073110518804211.

Becker, William C., and David A. Fiellin. 2020. "When Epidemics Collide: Coronavirus Disease 2019 (COVID-19) and the Opioid Crisis." *Annals of Internal Medicine.* https://doi.org/10.7326/m20-1210.

Boden, Sarah. 2018. "Carrick Could Be Site of City's Newest Needle Exchange." *WESA-FM*, September 13, 2018. https://www.wesa.fm/post/carrick-could-be-site-citys-newest-needle-exchange#stream/0.

Carroll, Jennifer J., Traci C. Green, and Rita K. Noonan. 2018. *Evidence-Based Strategies for Preventing Opioid Overdose: What's Working in the United States.* Atlanta: Centers for Disease Control and Prevention. https://www.cdc.gov/drugoverdose/pdf/pubs/2018-evidence-based-strategies.pdf.

Case, Anne, and Angus Deaton. 2020. *Deaths of Despair and the Future of Capitalism.* Princeton, NJ: Princeton University Press.

Cloud, William, and Robert Granfield. 2008. "Conceptualizing Recovery Capital: Expansion of a Theoretical Construct." *Substance Use & Misuse* 43, nos. 12–13: 1971–86. https://doi.org/10.1080/10826080802289762.

Department of Health and Human Services. 2018. *Naloxone: The Opioid Reversal Drug that Saves Lives.* Washington, DC: Department of Health and

Human Services. https://www.hhs.gov/opioids/sites/default/files/2018-12/naloxone-coprescribing-guidance.pdf.

de Quincey, Thomas. 1995. *Confessions of an English Opium Eater*. Mineola, NY: Dover Publications.

Diez Roux, Ana V. 2017. "Despair as a Cause of Death: More Complex Than It First Appears." *American Journal of Public Health* 107, no. 10: 1566–67. https://doi.org/10.2105/ajph.2017.304041.

Edin, Kathryn, Timothy Nelson, Andrew Cherlin, and Robert Francis. 2019. "The Tenuous Attachments of Working-Class Men." *Journal of Economic Perspectives* 33, no. 2: 211–28. https://doi.org/10.1257/jep.33.2.211.

Hoerr, John. 1988. *And the Wolf Finally Came: The Decline and Fall of the American Steel Industry*. Pittsburgh, PA: University of Pittsburgh Press.

Hulsey, Eric, Fizza Shah, Peter Jhon, LaToya Warren, and Erin Dalton. 2019. *Data Brief: Naloxone Distribution in the Allegheny County Jail to Prevent Overdose*. Pittsburgh, PA: Allegheny County Department of Human Services, Allegheny County Health Department and Allegheny County Jail. https://www.alleghenycountyanalytics.us/wp-content/uploads/2019/02/18-ACDHS-27-NaloxoneACJ-022119_v2.pdf.

Inagaki, Tristen K., Laura I. Hazlett, and Carmen Andreescu. 2019. "Naltrexone Alters Responses to Social and Physical Warmth: Implications for Social Bonding." *Social Cognitive and Affective Neuroscience* 14, no. 5: 471–79. https://doi.org/10.1093/scan/nsz026.

———. 2020. "Opioids and Social Bonding: Effect of Naltrexone on Feelings of Social Connection and Ventral Striatum Activity to Close Others." *Journal of Experimental Psychology: General* 149, no. 4: 732–45. https://doi.org/doi:10.1037/xge0000674.

Klinenberg, Eric. 2018. *Palaces for the People: How Social Infrastructure Can Help Fight Inequality, Polarization, and the Decline of Civic Life*. New York: Crown.

Kolla, Gillian, and Carol Strike. 2019. "'It's Too Much, I'm Getting Really Tired of It': Overdose Response and Structural Vulnerabilities among Harm Reduction Workers in Community Settings." *International Journal of Drug Policy* 74: 127–35. https://doi.org/10.1016/j.drugpo.2019.09.012.

Komro, Kelli A. 2018. "Preventing Risk for 'Deaths of Despair' among American Indian Youths: Unanswered Questions for Future Research." *American Journal of Public Health* 108, no. 8: 973–74. https://doi.org/10.2105/ajph.2018.304522.

Maier, Craig T. 2018. "Light and Shadows: Appreciative Inquiry, Communication Ethics Literacy, and the Opioid Epidemic." *Qualitative Research Reports in Communication* 19, no. 1: 62–67. https://doi.org/10.1080/17459435.2018.1529699.

Mason, Maryann, Sarah B. Welch, Ponni Arunkumar, Lori Ann Post, and Joseph M. Feinglass. 2021. "Notes from the Field: Opioid Overdose Deaths before, during, and after an 11-Week COVID-19 Stay-at-Home Order — Cook County, Illinois, January 1, 2018–October 6, 2020." *Morbidity and*

Mortality Weekly Report, 70: 362–63. https://doi.org/doi:10.15585/mmwr.mm7010a3.

McLean, Katherine. 2016. "There's Nothing Here": Deindustrialization as Risk Environment for Overdose. *International Journal of Drug Policy* 29: 19–26. https://doi.org/10.1016/j.drugpo.2016.01.009.

Muennig, Peter A., Megan Reynolds, David S. Fink, Zafar Zafari, and Arline T. Geronimus. 2018. "America's Declining Well-Being, Health, and Life Expectancy: Not Just a White Problem." *American Journal of Public Health* 108, no. 12: 1626–31. https://doi.org/10.2105/ajph.2018.304585.

National Institute on Drug Abuse. April 2020. "COVID-19: Potential Implications for Individuals with Substance Use Disorders." Accessed June 16, 2020. https://www.drugabuse.gov/about-nida/noras-blog/2020/04/covid-19-potential-implications-individuals-substance-use-disorders.

———. January 2021. "Overdose Death Rates." Accessed May 20, 2021. https://www.drugabuse.gov/related-topics/trends-statistics/overdose-death-rates#:~:text=Drug%20overdose%20deaths%20involving%20any%20opioid%E2%80%95prescription%20opioids%20(including%20methadone, among%20males%20(Figure%203).

Overdose Free PA. n.d. "View County Death Data." Accessed May 28, 2020. https://www.overdosefreepa.pitt.edu/know-the-facts/view-overdose-death-data.

Pennsylvania Department of Health. 2020. "Pennsylvania Opioid Data Dashboard." Accessed May 28, 2020. https://data.pa.gov/stories/s/9q45-nckt/.

Putnam, Robert. 2000. *Bowling Alone: The Collapse and Revival of American Community*. New York: Simon & Schuster.

Quinones, Sam. 2015. *Dreamland: The True Tale of America's Opiate Epidemic*. New York: Bloomsbury Press.

Rhodes, Tim. 2009. "Risk Environments and Drug Harms: A Social Science for Harm Reduction Approach." *International Journal of Drug Policy* 20, no. 3: 193–201. https://doi.org/10.1016/j.drugpo.2008.10.003.

Saloner, Brendan, Emma E. McGinty, Leo Beletsky, Ricky Bluthenthal, Chris Beyrer, Michael Botticelli, and Susan G. Sherman. 2018. "A Public Health Strategy for the Opioid Crisis." *Public Health Reports* 133, no. 1: 24S–34S. https://doi.org/10.1177/0033354918793627.

Sennett, Richard. 1998. *The Corrosion of Character*. New York: W. W. Norton & Company.

Shanahan, Lilly, Sherika N. Hill, Lauren M. Gaydosh, Annekatrin Steinhoff, E. Jane Costello, Kenneth A. Dodge, Kathleen M. Harris, and William E. Copeland. 2019. "Does Despair Really Kill? A Roadmap for an Evidence-Based Answer." *American Journal of Public Health* 109, no. 6: 854–58. https://doi.org/10.2105/AJPH.2019.305016.

Simpson, Vicki. 2020. "Community Resilience: One Community's View of Recovery from the Opioid Epidemic." *International Journal of Community Well-Being*. https://doi.org/10.1007/s42413-020-00064-9.

Tsai, Alexander C., Mathew V. Kiang, Michael L. Barnett, Leo Beletsky, Katherine M. Keyes, Emma E. McGinty, Laramie R. Smith, Steffanie A. Strathdee, Sarah E. Wakeman, and Atheendar S. Venkataramani. 2019. "Stigma as a Fundamental Hindrance to the United States Opioid Overdose Crisis Response." *PLOS Medicine* 16, no. 11: e1002969. https://doi.org/10.1371/journal.pmed.1002969.

Zoorob, Michael J., and Jason L. Salemi. 2017. "Bowling Alone, Dying Together: The Role of Social Capital in Mitigating the Drug Overdose Epidemic in the United States." *Drug and Alcohol Dependence* 173: 1–9. https://doi.org/10.1016/j.drugalcdep.2016.12.011.

2 The Challenge of Communal Literacy

In *Bowling Alone*, Robert Putnam (2000) both describes the importance of social capital and worries that Americans are pulling back from institutions that build and sustain this essential resource. Granted, some have found Putnam's conceptualization of social capital hazy, his explanation of the causes of its decline—a mixture of suburban sprawl, rampant consumerism, and television—inconclusive, and the consequences of declining civic engagement hard to quantify (see, for instance, Durlauf 2002). And as critics of communitarianism might contend (see, for instance, Phillips 1993), Putnam's lament over the decline of "community" can often lead to calls to return, seemingly by force, to idealized pasts that never existed or institutional structures defined by deep social injustice. In other words, there could be very good reasons why Americans might not want to participate in local bowling leagues, and the demise of these particular associations might actually be a good thing.

Yet, as the previous chapter argued, the dynamics Putnam discussed two decades ago are even more true today and appear to be playing a role in shaping the macro-level risk environment that gives rise to opioid use disorder (McLean 2016; Zoorob and Salemi 2017). If we are concerned about the opioid epidemic, then we also need to be concerned about the quality of social connection and the effects of its absence on American life. And this concern reaches beyond opioids: Eric Klinenberg (2018) argues that the declines in social connection, reciprocity, and trust that so concern Putnam are omnipresent in contemporary American society and limit our capacity to deliberate about and respond to the profoundly complex racial, environmental, political, and social problems we face together. Of course, recognizing the problems posed by low social connection, reciprocity, and trust is not the same as proposing a response. This chapter explores the problem through the metaphor of what it calls *communal literacy*, first by discussing its relevance and then by framing it as a construct.

DOI: 10.4324/9781003243663-3

The Context of Communal Literacy

Framing the problem of American social life in terms of "literacy"—or, even worse, "illiteracy"—seems to conjure up all of the worst fears of communitarianism's critics. In particular, it suggests forms of remedial moral education imposed from above by dour schoolmasters whose credentials we never get to question. Indeed, Putnam's (2000) uneasiness of the state of American social capital, Alasdair MacIntyre's (2007) worries about the rise of extreme polarization in American society emerging from irreconcilable ethical disagreements, Robert Bellah and his colleagues' (1985, 1991) concerns regarding the effects of excessive individualism on American institutions, and Charles Taylor's (1992) distress over the increasing sense of disconnection in contemporary life from traditional sources of identity and meaning all share a common theme of deficit and loss that brings with it a sense of nostalgia, fear, and guilt. While all of their observations are likely true—political polarization is now a central social problem in the United States, American institutions ranging from local police departments and schools to the Roman Catholic Church and the Centers for Disease Control and Prevention all seem to be on the brink of failure, and society increasingly feels unmoored and adrift—the troubling feelings their arguments engender seem to be the worst places from which to mount a response. Nostalgia, fear, and guilt, after all, cannot make the past reappear on its own. And as Isaac Catt (2000) reminds us, calls to restore the past both assume that the past is worth restoring and woefully overestimate the ability of our network of barely functioning institutions to make this so.

Moreover, nostalgia, fear, and guilt may not be necessary. Klinenberg (2018), for instance, emphasizes the importance of what he calls *social infrastructure* in recovering social capital. Klinenberg's definition of social infrastructure is expansive, including everything from sidewalks, parks, and athletic fields to libraries, schools, and farmers' markets to community gardens, cafes, and barbershops—any space where strangers are forced to encounter, interact with, and learn to relate to each other. "When social infrastructure is robust, it fosters contact, mutual support, and collaboration among friends and neighbors," he writes in *Palaces for the People*. "When degraded, it inhibits social activity, leaving families and individuals to fend for themselves" (2018, 5). For Klinenberg, social capital grows naturally from the built environment. When strangers congregate in a new playground, he suggests, the innate human impulse for social connection enables them to find ways to overcome the things that separate them, and social capital grows as naturally as the grass under their feet. As a result, instead of looking backward with regret, we need to invest in building social spaces in the same way we need to devote resources to building bridges and sewers.

Klinenberg's (2018) recommendations are important, especially for places like Southton and countless other neighborhoods and towns throughout the United States suffering from blight and neglect. Moreover, the investments that he recommends offer a forward-looking way of growing social capital, in which we are not looking to recapture a lost past but building new spaces where people can grow into the future together. Nevertheless, even Klinenberg himself recognizes that the problem is much more complex than his argument suggests, and not just because devoting resources to building and maintaining *any* kind of infrastructure is something that the United States has found increasingly impossible to do. For instance, while Klinenberg praises social media for its ability to allow people, especially those experiencing marginalization and hostility in the offline world, to connect over vast distances, he also recognizes that these platforms are no substitute for face-to-face interaction. "As meaningful as the friendships we establish online can be," he writes, "most of us are unsatisfied with virtual ties that never develop into face-to-face relationships" (2018, 42). Even as people are starved for relational contact, he continues, the disembodied nature of digital communication and virtual public spaces can translate into toxic behaviors and polarized, insular social worlds that leave people bruised and wary. Even though he is sanguine about people's abilities ultimately to overcome these difficulties, Klinenberg also suggests that social media all too often serves as an *anti-social* infrastructure that offers a pseudo-form of social connectedness while simultaneously inculcating habits of thought and mind that make the experience of real community—offline and online—increasingly difficult.

The challenge extends beyond social media. Anne Case and Angus Deaton (2020) remind us that the American economy itself increasingly values relentless competition over cooperation, forcing everyone into a ruthless zero-sum game with a shrinking number of winners and an ever-expanding number of losers. Zygmunt Bauman (2000) has described this process as a sort of social liquefaction, in which the clear social strata of the twentieth century are starting to melt, with the winners evaporating off to jet around in a stateless stratosphere, the losers—whose numbers are disproportionately Black and brown but, as the experience of Southton suggests, also include an increasing number of working-class whites—sliding down into the abyss, and a frantic upper middle class hoarding their economic, social, cultural, and educational resources and privileges at all costs, even if it means pushing everyone else down. Such an environment, as Richard Sennett (2006) writes, drowns the foundation for social cooperation and connection in a sea of toxic *ressentiment*. Even if social cooperation does occur, he argues, it gives rise to transient public relationships defined by omnipresent fear: fear of making a mistake in a game people increasingly believe is rigged for them to lose, fear of losing what they have, and, most of all, fear of being declared useless and worthless without any recourse or appeal. Such a climate, where social anxiety is not a pathology but a necessary adaptation to reality, turns social isolation into a survival strategy.

Sennett's (1998, 2006) and Bauman's (2000) work speaks to a third element complicating community life: the increasing sense of social and economic precarity felt by many Americans, even those whose race, income, education level, and zip code would give us little reason to expect that they are living under such stress. To be precarious, as Andrew Ross (2009) writes, means that one feels that they must beg (from the Latin *precare*) in order to survive. He argues that the ranks of precarious persons—the *precariat*—are expanding, including not only traditionally marginalized populations but also migrants and displaced persons, the growing numbers of "essential workers" living hand-to-mouth in the gig economy, and even highly educated and well-paid "micro-serfs" working on short-term contracts with no benefits and little expectation of loyalty from the start-ups working them 100 hours per week (see also Sennett 1998, 2006). Guy Standing (2014) observes that the first casualty of living such a precarious life is the leisure to breathe, relax, and think. This stress and exhaustion, he continues, leads to anger from the deep frustrations the precariat experience, anomie that insulates them from the constant drumbeat of failure they hear, anxiety over their declining prospects and uncertain future, and alienation resulting from the feeling that they are constantly being betrayed or fooled by those in power. Left unattended, he concludes, precarity leads to what he calls a *politics of inferno* that quickly consumes—figuratively and, perhaps, even literally—everything that it touches, including the social infrastructure that might create and sustain social capital.

The inability to control the stresses of precarity creates a fourth and final element that complicates the development of social connection and capital: the widespread experience of both individual and community-level trauma. As Bessel van der Kolk (2014) notes, traumatic experiences are disturbingly commonplace in contemporary

American society. On an individual level, adverse childhood experiences of losing a parent or family member, losing a loved one struggling with substance use disorder, growing up amidst structural racism and homophobia, or being physically, emotionally, or sexually abused can have tremendous effects on how a person communicates and builds relationships as an adult. To this list, we might also add the cumulative effects of living the sorts of precarious lives that Ross (2009) and Standing (2014) describe, the constant stress of being pushed beyond one's limits without hope of rest and recuperation. And we can add living with the chronic stress and uncertainty of the coronavirus pandemic, which may be remembered as a slow-moving trauma event with long-term implications for nearly all Americans. Those with histories of trauma, van der Kolk argues, behave in ways that seem strange to observers, lashing out aggressively at the slightest provocation, fleeing social relationships, or becoming passive and disengaged when under stress. Since none of these reactions is conducive to constructive public relationships and social connection, the proliferation of trauma events at the individual level seems poised to make interpersonal and group communication increasingly difficult for decades to come.

But as Rachel Davis, Howard Pinderhughes, and Myesha Williams (2016) contend, people can also experience trauma at the community level. They argue that the chronic presence of violence, systemic racism, substance use disorders, economic misery, dilapidated buildings, environmental hazards, poor schools, and countless other social problems—all of which are magnified through the society-level trauma of the COVID-19 pandemic—show up in broken social relationships, poor physical health, frayed social networks, increased interpersonal and physical violence, and a climate of hopelessness and apathy. In this sense, the relational toxicity in Southton and the surrounding communities described in the previous chapter—the stigmatizing behaviors of medical staff toward people who had just survived overdoses, the feelings of disengagement and despair among first responders, and the unexpectedly aggressive response of residents to the proposal of a needle exchange van—take on a deeper resonance (Maier 2018). All of these things suggest a deeper pattern of individual and community-level trauma stretching back to the collapse of the steel economy in the 1980s that continues to influence how people relate to each other (Hoerr 1988).

These problems call to mind the challenges of the early decades of the twentieth century when industrialization and urbanization were presenting a host of complex problems within American society. Writing in the 1920s, John Dewey (1991) argued against the belief that American public life had come apart amidst the strains of contemporary life. The public, he argued, was not a "phantom," as some believed (Lippmann 1993), but merely "bewildered" (1991, 116). In a similar way, we can argue that the potential for community and connection in the United States remains as strong as it was in Dewey's time, but it faces challenges that Dewey never envisioned. The public remains just as bewildered, but it is also polarized, distracted, frightened, exhausted, stressed, and angry at the precarious and chronically traumatic realities that now define American life. This seems true even of a predominantly white neighborhood like Southton and the communities that surround it, where decades of economic decline and the opioid epidemic conspire to create a climate of stigmatization, frustration, and despair among residents and between residents and the institutional authorities trying to help them. In such a situation, the intensive social infrastructure program Klinenberg (2018) demands—no matter how necessary, well-intentioned, and well-designed it may be—seems insufficient to produce the social capital areas like Southton need. What is required is a new form of civic education that works alongside these investments to help residents improve how they communicate with each other. But where Dewey and his followers focused on forums where a bewildered public could learn to grapple with the challenges it faced (Keith 2007), the challenges of civic education today are much more fundamental. The construct of *communal literacy* speaks to this need.

Communal Literacy and the Search for the Great Community

For Dewey (1991), the test of a democracy lies in the ability of its people to become a Great Community where people have learned to balance an interest in the autonomous "I" with a commitment to a broader sense of "We." But what is this "We"? To be sure, Dewey's conception of community, inspired by both the New England town hall meeting and the assumptions of progressive civic education (Keith 2007), presupposes a sort of cultural homogeneity that bears no resemblance to contemporary American society—and, truth be told, ignores the perspective of anyone other than upper middle class, white men. The notion of "community," we know now, can mean many different things, from comfortable social sameness defined by consumerism and conformity (Bellah et al. 1985) to webs of relationships rooted in commitments to ultimate values (Weil 1952) to much darker visions defined by ideological purity, fear of outsiders, and defensive walls to keep the "borders" intact (Bauman 2000). Although these definitions of community differ, all of them share a common assumption that a community is or should be permanent in some way, although they differ as to what that permanence should be. Here, the definitions of community, as well as the communities that hold them, can run aground. Focusing on the wrong sort of permanence—ethnic homogeneity, emotional comfort, consumption patterns, ideological purity—can obviously lead to trouble. But even more important are our assumptions about permanence itself. Grounding our sense of "We" in a way of life that requires the world to remain just so in order for our community to function means that if we want to keep a community healthy, we need to find a way to keep the world from changing, an endeavor that is both impossible and harmful for everyone involved.

Ronald C. Arnett (2005) suggests an alternative grounding of community grounded not in the permanence of a particular culture, idea, place, or set of relationships but in the communication among its members. Writing on Dietrich Bonhoeffer's struggle to sustain a community capable of resisting the horrors of Nazi Germany, Arnett advances a vision of community as a *communicative home* grounded in a story that draws members together. Such a story, he continues, situates them within a "context (historical situation), plot (direction), main characters (embedded agents), and events that capture and maintain [their] attention (communicative practices)" (2005, 38). As Alasdair MacIntyre (2007) suggests, these stories are vital because they provide a sort of container in which community can arise. "I can only answer the question 'What am I to do?'" MacIntyre (2007, 216) writes, "if I can answer the prior question 'Of what story or stories do I find myself a part?'" But while the story is important, we cannot confuse the container with the communicative home dwelling inside it. A communicative home, in a sense, is the story people choose to tell about the story in which they live: how they choose to interpret it, retell it, live it, debate it, and change it over time. What is permanent in a community, then, is not the story but the group's conversation about the story, the ways they choose to live this conversation, and their commitment to keeping this conversation going (Rorty 1979). *In this sense, we can define a community as a group of people engaged in a conversation about a story that matters.*

The notion of *story*, as Arnett (2005) and MacIntyre (2007) are using it here, differs from that of *narrative*, which connotes a much deeper sense of cultural grounding (Arnett, Fritz, and McManus 2018). In the past, the narratives found in the great religious, spiritual, and ethical traditions served as moral sources (Taylor 1992) that gave individual and social life continuity and purpose. Since the Enlightenment, however, these narratives have gradually eroded in significance. Some of this decline has been welcome, especially when it has eased sectarian violence and promoted reasoned debate and democratic institutions. Nevertheless, Arnett, writing with Janie M. Harden Fritz and Leanne M. Bell McManus (2018), suggests that the Enlightenment's success in dethroning traditional narratives has also unintentionally engendered a deep sense of confusion that is increasingly threatening the very liberal order the Enlightenment sought to create. Without a generally accepted account of what a good life looks like, what makes a community thrive, or what constitutes knowledge, contemporary humanity has lost its sense of what Arnett and his colleagues call *narrative ground.* Beliefs once understood to be common sense no longer hold, making social life slippery and uncertain. Arnett, Fritz, and McManus suggest that in such a moment, stories become crucial to finding our footing. Though they lack the transcendent power of narrative, stories offer accounts of the world that are just coherent enough to help us make sense of our lives (Fisher 1987). To maintain this coherence, stories need to be practiced, retold, and renewed. This practicing, retelling, and renewal drive the conversation that brings a community to life.

Living this conversation, however, requires a fundamental transformation in the quality of the interactions among a community's members. Dewey (1991) argues that a group of people, even a group as large as a nation and spanning an entire continent like the United States, can function well on *transactions* of money, goods, information, and ideas—at least for a time. But while Margaret Thatcher's brand of advanced capitalism contends that transactions are the best we can hope for (Keay 1987), Dewey believes a Great Community must reach much deeper:

> Human associations may be ever so organic in origin and firm in operation, but they develop into societies in a human sense only as their consequences, being known, are esteemed and sought for. Even if "society" were as much an organism as some writers have held, it would not on that account be society. Interactions, transactions, occur *de facto* and the results of interdependence follow. But participation in activities and sharing in results are additive concerns. They demand *communication* as a prerequisite.
>
> (1991, 152)

In advocating a movement from transaction to communication, Dewey sketches nothing less than an outline of the discipline of communication studies as practiced in the United States. But where the problems the public had to address in the years before the Great Depression were large, they seem to pale in comparison to the challenges that Americans face today. Even more important, Dewey's bewildered public, as tainted by structural racism, sexism, and classism as it was, still could rely on basic institutional structures, commonly held conversational norms, and a working consensus on facts. Today, the way from transaction to communication is far less clear than it would have been for Dewey, requiring a far more nuanced and reflexive understanding of communication than he would ever have foreseen.

The field of communication ethics steps into that gap, helping people reflect on the institutions and norms that guide how people communicate with each other, especially in moments where disagreement is so deep that nothing can bridge it. Arnett, Fritz, and McManus (2018) note that, much like the notion of community, people can define communication ethics in any number of ways—as codes of professional communication conduct, for instance, norms of civil discourse, conversational etiquette, an ethical demand to listen to the Other, and so on—and that each of these understandings can have important implications for how we communicate. Yet, as Deborah Eicher-Catt (2013) observes, such definitions, while helpful, often ignore important questions of inequality and exclusion or, as is sometimes the case in calls to maintain "civility," serve as excuses for marginalizing ideas, perspectives, and persons disruptive to the status quo. As a result, Eicher-Catt contends that communication ethics must go deeper than defining standards of "niceness" to engage in the messy labor of communication itself.

Arnett and his colleagues (2018) understand this labor as protecting and promoting the *goods* a community's stories engender. Goods—a term that includes not only fundamental ideals, norms, and institutions but also the assets a community desires to protect, as well as its hopes, goals, and vision for the future—represent a sort of crystallization of the values a community's stories explicitly or implicitly hold. A well-known folktale about a witch who punishes a family for hoarding food during a crisis, for instance, may encourage a community to prize compassion. A local history about the efforts of teachers and students to integrate a school may underscore the importance of education, as well as the good embodied in the school building itself. The memories of a heroic activist's life may give birth to a vision that still inspires a community decades later. These goods—compassion, education, the school, the hope-filled vision—provide touchpoints that make ethical conversations possible. Simply demanding that people not speak over one another, tell the truth as best they know it, or refrain from hurtful or demeaning language is insufficient. People need to know *how* these practices protect and promote the social goods that further their lives together. Even more important, they need to understand the stories that tell them *why* these goods are worth the effort. And most important of all, they need to know *that* these goods exist in the first place.

Arnett and his colleagues' (2018) work points to a working definition of communication ethics *as a field that acknowledges and interrogates the stories and social goods at work in our lives together, considers communicative practices that protect and promote those stories and goods, and explores how those practices can support the communicative homes necessary for flourishing communities.* Today, they contend, such a field is increasingly urgent within a diverse and divided American society. Indeed, framing communication ethics in this way suggests that both the collapse of intelligible communities and Americans' impotence in rejuvenating their public life are unsurprising given Americans' willful ignorance of each other's stories and inability to come to any sort of meaningful agreement regarding the existence of social goods at all, let alone their ability to prioritize these goods or translate them into practices they can share. The rot, in short, goes all the way down. This realization suggests, once again, that Klinenberg's (2018) belief that social infrastructure alone can create the Great Community Dewey (1991) envisions is unduly optimistic. A community absolutely needs social infrastructure, but it also requires an ability to navigate diversity and conflict and a commitment to showing up for one another when the situation demands.

Perhaps the most important way we "show up" for each other is through dialogue. For this reason, communication ethics pays particular attention to dialogic ethics. Although we often assume that "dialogue" is synonymous with long, heartfelt conversations leading to a blissful meeting of minds, hearts, and souls (Peters 1999), Arnett, Fritz, and McManus (2018) advance a dialogic ethic grounded in a more nuanced understanding of relational engagement, in which radically different people learn from each other under extraordinary complexity and pressure. Drawing from Martin Buber (1955), they observe that dialogic ethics recognizes that dialogue is but one way in which we communicate with others and build strong relationships. At some points, the deep meeting of dialogue is important, but at others, the *monologue* of bearing witness to one's own experiences or what Buber calls the *technical dialogue* of exchanging information about a topic of common concern may be more vital. For this reason, Arnett and his coauthors (2018) suggest that dialogic ethics begins in irony: *The first move of dialogic ethics is to decenter dialogue itself to focus instead on the needs of the situation and the Other.* Instead of requiring persons to relate to each other in a particular way, dialogic ethics unfolds in what Hans-Georg Gadamer (1976, 2004) would describe as a playful spirit that recognizes the value of the entire continuum of ways people build and maintain relationships with each other. Dialogic ethics, then, is open, experimental, and dynamic, constantly aware of a multiplicity of ethical perspectives and ways of communicating. It calls us, as Arnett and his colleagues (2018, 248) put it, to "listen without demand" in order to open spaces where community can form.

Arnett and his colleagues (2018) argue that this playfulness is not an end unto itself. Dialogic ethics, they argue, should generate learning, not intimacy or coziness. Following Hannah Arendt (1978), they remind us that there will always be relational spaces that are so different that we do not, cannot, and will never feel completely "at home" or that we "belong." In these encounters of radical difference, dialogic ethics seeks what Gadamer (1976) calls a *fusion of horizons* in which different perspectives learn to discover each other on their own terms. For such learning to occur, however, participants must recognize that learning is both necessary and possible. "Learning presupposes that we have something to learn that is different from our current knowledge base," Arnett and his coauthors (2018, 85) observe. "Dialogue is a mechanism for such learning." Paulo Freire (2000), whose work on action research will become vital later, contends that such learning requires extraordinary vulnerability, in which those coming from standpoints of privilege must step down from their pedestals to open themselves to the challenges from below, while those coming from below take the risk of bearing witness to what they understand the world to be. But again, embracing equality does not mean that the privileged and the oppressed will resolve their differences—or that dialogue has failed if does not end in mutual understanding. As Lisbeth Lipari (2014) emphasizes, a dialogue that reveals the depth of our misunderstanding is actually *more* successful because it shows us how much we have to learn and calls us to listen more closely to each other. This realization opens a second rich irony: *Dialogic ethics does not facilitate mutual understanding as much as it helps persons navigate misunderstanding.* And because misunderstanding seems to be the natural state of human social existence, dialogic ethics' capacity for negotiating difference makes it indispensable for life together.

Dialogic ethics, then, charts a challenging course for those longing for community. Perhaps understandably, then, Arnett, Fritz, and McManus (2018) contend that today, as American society becomes ever more polarized and the perils it faces ever more demanding, we cannot assume that Americans have the skills to negotiate public spaces and respond to the difficulties they find there. As a result, the commitment to building social infrastructure that Klinenberg (2018) advocates requires an equally strong commitment to helping people learn how to be in community again. Arnett and his co-authors describe this learning as a form of *ethical literacy*. Focusing on *ethics*, as opposed to morality, they describe communication ethics as an open-ended field concerned with helping people learn and understand the stories and goods at stake in a given situation, not a close-minded field preoccupied with policing what people should or should not say or do. In a moment when disagreement over fundamental norms and values within American public life is high, and when the traumas and strains of American private life are increasingly impossible to bear, a commitment to *literacy*, or learning, is an essential first step. Instead of beginning from a place of judgment, a commitment to literacy puts ethical reflection on the ground, helping to surface and name the conflicting stories and values in play. Instead of looking to the past as offering laws to settle present disagreements once and for all, it engages the present to help people who may never agree find ways to work, live, and solve problems together.

Arnett and his colleagues' (2018) conception of ethical literacy is a much broader construct that operates in a variety of domains, from interpersonal and relational communication to organizational and intercultural communication. *Communal literacy*, as understood here, extends ethical literacy by connecting it intentionally to the practice of community life. Previously, the term "communal literacy" has typically been used to refer to how living and being within a particular community shapes how its members learn to read and write (see Wynter-Hoyte and Boutte 2018; Seward 2019) or influences the practice of reading, writing, and interpreting information (see Kapitzke 1995; Kauhanen-Simanainen 2007; McNamara 2007; Vandi 2015). Communal literacy, in the context of this study, will be used differently. Instead of viewing communal literacy as the way in which social forces influence how people communicate, this study reverses the relationship, emphasizing how people negotiate and build community through their communication. Just as traditional understandings of literacy encompass both an ability to read texts and an ability to write new ones, and ethical literacy involves the ability to understand and negotiate the complex conflicts over values that surround us, *communal literacy involves an ability to understand and respect what matters most to those around us and, based on that understanding, to discover, create, and sustain new forms of community that allow everyone to flourish.*

In this sense, communal literacy reflects a fundamental capacity to participate in social life constructively. Unlike communitarian approaches that may operate from a misplaced nostalgia or a desire to force one type of ideal community into being at the expense of others, communal literacy is grounded in inquiry that draws people into conversation with each other about what they hope to be together. In other words, communal literacy seeks to be forward-looking, not backward-looking, in shaping community life. But at the same time, it echoes Dewey's (1991) admonition that moving from transaction to communication requires attention and intention from everyone involved.

Arnett and his co-authors' (2018) conception of ethical literacy suggests that communal literacy contains several facets. To begin with, it includes an ability to recognize the various stories and goods in play within a community. Because different groups will have different interests and different histories, they will value different goods or understand the same good differently than others. As a result, Arnett and his colleagues contend, recognizing stories and goods also entails acknowledging the various ways they come into conflict. A Quaker who is a committed pacifist, for instance, is communally literate if they recognize the values of loyalty, patriotism, and duty that compel their neighbor to join the Marines, and they can also find it in themselves to respect the story of the Marine Corps as an institution, even if they abhor war on principle. Likewise, their neighbor will be communally literate to the degree they can appreciate the pacifist's Quaker heritage and recognize the importance of nonviolent problem-solving, even if they strongly believe that nonviolence has limits in a cruel and unjust world. This mutual acknowledgment does not require the Quaker and the Marine to agree with each other completely or fully understand why they think and act as they do, but it does help them navigate their complex relationship so they can live and work together.

We will call this capacity for respectful awareness *attending to what matters*. As *The Good Society* (Bellah et al. 1991) suggests, a flourishing democracy requires people to pay attention to the stories and goods around them, instead of simply focusing on their own needs and priorities. And many stories and goods warrant our attention. On an institutional level, goods emerge from what Bellah and his colleagues describe as the core institutional fields that they believe define American life: its schools, legal system, economy, political life, and religious association. But this by no means exhausts the list of things that matter to a community. On an intercultural level, they come from differences in race, ethnicity, and culture, the intricate and often dark histories that come with these differences, and commitments that might transcend these differences. Finally, on an interpersonal level, they arise from things like gender identity and sexual orientation, as well as seemingly ordinary lifestyle choices like veganism and recycling practices that Ulrich Beck (1994) sees as having an increasingly public, political dimension.

Although these goods are quite different from each other, Arnett and his colleagues (2018) note that each is embedded within a story that gives it significance and context. Moreover, these stories interact with each other in nuanced ways, as individual and group histories intertwine. Being communally literate means knowing how these stories intersect and influence each other, the goods that emerge from this interaction, the ways goods change or become more or less important over time, and how different goods create both tensions and opportunities for agreement.

But as Arnett, Fritz, and McManus (2018) contend, paying attention to what matters is much more than simply knowing where the fault lines are and how to negotiate those lines. Stories and goods *compete* as well as *conflict*, in two ways. To begin with, two or more people can believe in the same story or value the same good but interpret them differently. When it comes to the good of education, for instance, the Quaker may emphasize the importance of learning to think for oneself or appreciate diversity, while the Marine may see schooling as leading to concrete job skills. Here, such a difference may at times bring a new sort of conflict, in which they agree on the goal but disagree on how to get there or why the goal is worth pursuing. Alongside this difficulty, stories and goods compete in the sense that a particular situation may require us to hold multiple stories or goods at the same time and find some sort of accommodation between them. To continue the example, the Quaker and the Marine may both recognize that a good education requires balancing a commitment to the good of academic rigor with a commitment to the good of children's emotional and social well-being. And so when it comes to how much homework to assign a third grader or how much importance a standardized test should have on a teenager's life chances, the Quaker and the Marine may find themselves on the same side of the debate but confused about where to proceed. In all of these cases, attending to these gaps reflects much more than documentary interest. We need to know how to *nurse* them, entering into their tensions through a practice of gentle probing and tending with the knowledge that we cannot heal the divide by trying to force it closed (Christensen, Morsing, and Thyssen 2013).

Beyond this ability to "read" and "understand" different ethical standpoints, communal literacy also encompasses the ability to "do" community through one's relationships with others. For Arnett and his co-authors (2018), communal literacy also includes understanding how and why to show up for the sake of the community when the situation demands. We will call this capacity *being present* to others for the sake of the community as a whole. For instance, we might say that the Quaker and the Marine are communally literate if they can set aside their differences long enough to participate in local community events, listen to each other in substantive conversations about issues that concern them both, or come to the other's need in times of distress, even when it might be inconvenient, uncomfortable, or painful to do so.

As Arnett and his colleagues (2018) note, being present requires some level of effort and discipline. In a time of constant distraction and stress, it can be difficult to show up and support others when the situation demands it. But being present can also take a variety of forms. For communities struggling with legacies of trauma that make participation uncomfortable or even frightening in some cases, or for individuals whose economic and social precarity denies them the leisure to take part as fully as they would like, being present can look quite different. As a result, just as the goods that a community protects and promotes must be understood to change over time, the norms for participation must also be flexible and attuned to the situation. A communally literate person, then, understands how to be present without demand, engaging others while making space for others to engage as their needs and abilities permit.

Finally, communal literacy involves the ability to recognize and care for what Arnett and his colleagues (2018) call the *common centers* that allow people who may believe themselves to be utterly different from one another to find spaces of commonality, however small they may be. Common centers are important, they argue, because of how these spaces call people together. The Quaker and the Marine, for instance, may have occasions to bond over their mutual love of their children's Little League team, even as they might disagree on everything else. Serving as a form of social infrastructure (Klinenberg 2018) that builds social capital (Putnam 2000), the team thus serves a vital social importance within the community. But it also requires care to survive and thrive. In this sense, the Quaker and the Marine are communally literate if they both understand the importance of this league in their lives together *and* devote themselves to preserving it.

We will call this facet of communal literacy *caring for the common.* Through it, community members reach outward and upward, preserving the spaces, places, and institutions that draw them together around particular social goods. Eicher-Catt (2013) describes these acts of care as a form of semiotic labor that serves what she calls the *good of the common*. Where appeals to the "common good" tend to assume that a community requires consensus around a single set of values and falls apart when that sense of fundamental agreement falters, seeing community as the "good of the common"—that is, something that calls people together despite their differences—suggests that the potential for community can still exist even if consensus can never be reached. This is because institutional "commons," such as the goods they hold together, are owned by no one in particular but are instead the property of the group. In the classroom, for instance, trying to "own" the subject being studied or "control" the discussion and learning environment is a recipe for disaster because it closes the system and makes it impossible to draw in new information and ideas (Karolak and Maier 2015). Caring for the common tends to the spaces where communication occurs so the conversation can continue (Rorty 1979).

These three capacities—attending to what matters, being present, caring for the common—could be understood to represent the "ABCs" of communal literacy. Together, this conceptual alphabet translates into a host of behaviors that allow communities to flourish. Through attending to what matters, communal literacy allows people to build relationships even if they disagree with each other, reinterpret or redefine the values they cherish, or propose new social goods that offer a new foundation for their lives together. Through being present, communal literacy reflects a capacity to build relationships with others and participate in community life across divides. Through caring for the common, communal literacy enables people to work together to preserve the social infrastructure from which community can arise. As Eicher-Catt (2013) would emphasize, communal literacy cannot guarantee the existence of a community. Rather, it represents a fundamental capacity that is essential for a community to emerge.

Certainly, the incidence of absolute communal illiteracy is low. Klinenberg (2018) is right to suggest that humans are social beings primed for connection, and as the stories of heroic acts of kindness and solidarity that have emerged repeatedly throughout the coronavirus pandemic have revealed, people can rise to the occasion when the community is in deep need or distress. But the rate of *functional* communal illiteracy today in a polarized American society seems much higher. Where functionally illiterate people can read and write but do so too slowly and painfully to participate fully in economic or social life, people who are functionally communally illiterate may know how to live in community but struggle to do so. They may be able to wax poetically about "common values," for instance, but find it hard to employ those values in their workplaces, in their churches and community groups, or online. Instead of showing up when the situation demands it, they may be comfortable engaging others only within gated communities or social "bubbles"—what Robert Bellah and his colleagues (1985) called *lifestyle enclaves*—where everyone believes the same way they do. Or they may not know what to do to keep the conversation going when difficulty arises and, as a result, do nothing.

Yet, even as we might cringe with self-recognition, the lack of communal literacy that so affects contemporary American life, just like traditional forms of illiteracy, is not the fault of laziness or stupidity. Just as the inability to read and write well is the product of a host of environmental factors over which we have little control, deficits in communal literacy are the natural consequence of living in dysfunctional societies where healthy community is neither practiced nor taught. This suggests a series of crucial but humbling questions. Although many people might be able to articulate what they value as individuals, how well can they acknowledge the values of others? After years of bowling alone—and months of high to moderate social distancing—how equipped are they for the hard work of being in community? And if living in a community teaches us how to live in community with others, how can we learn these lessons if the "school" is in disrepair? These questions cut to the heart of public discourse in our time, and answering them is essential for fulfilling Dewey's (1991) unrealized vision of the Great Community in American life.

Searching for the Great Community represents what Zaid Hassan (2014) calls a *complex challenge*. Our ability to answer the questions communal literacy poses depends on a whole host of socioeconomic, political, and cultural factors, not to mention the individual differences and histories each member of the community brings to the table. The conversation that arises from those differences—and the injustices, pains, frustrations, hopes, and loves just under the surface of those differences—constantly changes as every member of the community adapts to the environment around them. Police violence, plant closures, natural disasters, pandemics, wars, and technological change introduce new energies into the social system, to which each individual member will respond differently. In the face of such complexity, Hassan argues, top-down, technocratic solutions are not only of little use but can actually do more harm than good. Communal literacy, if it is to be renewed, must emerge from the bottom-up. Participatory Community Inquiry (PCI) strives to facilitate this growth.

References

Arendt, Hannah. 1978. *The Jew as Pariah: Jewish Identity and Politics in the Modern Age.* Edited by Ron H. Feldman. New York: Grove Press.

Arnett, Ronald C. 2005. *Dialogic Confession: Bonhoeffer's Rhetoric of Responsibility.* Carbondale: Southern Illinois University Press.

Arnett, Ronald C., Janie M. Harden Fritz, and Leeanne M. Bell McManus. 2018. *Communication Ethics Literacy: Dialogue and Difference.* 2nd ed. Dubuque, IA: Kendall Hunt Publishing.

Bauman, Zygmunt. 2000. *Liquid Modernity.* Malden, MA: Polity.

Beck, Ulrich. 1994. "The Reinvention of Politics: Towards a Theory of Reflexive Modernization." In *Reflexive Modernization: Politics, Tradition, and Aesthetics in the Modern Social Order,* edited by Ulrich Beck, Anthony Giddens, and Scott Lash, 1–55. Malden, MA: Polity.

Bellah, Robert N., Richard Madsen, William M. Sullivan, Ann Swidler, and Steven M. Tipton. 1985. *Habits of the Heart: Individualism and Commitment in American Life.* Berkeley: University of California Press.

———. 1991. *The Good Society.* New York: Vintage.

Buber, Martin. 1955. *Between Man and Man.* Translated by Ronald Gregor Smith. Boston, MA: Beacon Press.

Case, Anne, and Angus Deaton. 2020. *Deaths of Despair and the Future of Capitalism.* Princeton, NJ: Princeton University Press.

Catt, Isaac C. 2000. "The Institution of Communitarianism and the Communicology of Pierre Bourdieu." *The American Journal of Semiotics* 15, no. 1: 187–206. https://doi.org/10.5840/ajs200015/161/47.

Christensen, Lars Thøger, Mette Morsing, and Ole Thyssen. 2013. "CSR as Aspirational Talk." *Organization* 20, no. 3: 372–93. https://doi.org/10.1177/1350508413478310.

Davis, Rachel, Howard Pinderhughes, and Myesha Williams. 2016. *Adverse Community Experiences and Resilience: A Framework for Addressing and Preventing Community Trauma.* Oakland, CA: Prevention Institute.

Dewey, John. 1991. *The Public and Its Problems.* Athens, OH: Swallow Press.

Durlauf, Steven N. 2002. "Bowling Alone: A Review Essay." *Journal of Economic Behavior & Organization* 47, no. 3: 259–73. https://doi.org/10.1016/s0167-2681(01)00210-4.

Eicher-Catt, Deborah. 2013. "A Semiotic Interpretation of Authentic Civility: Preserving the Ineffable for the Good of the Common." *Communication Quarterly* 61, no. 1: 1–17. https://doi.org/10.1080/01463373.2012.718727.

Fisher, Walter R. 1987. *Human Communication as Narration: Toward a Philosophy of Reason, Value, and Action.* Columbia: University of South Carolina Press.

Freire, Paulo. 2000. *Pedagogy of the Oppressed.* 30th anniversary ed. New York: Continuum.

Gadamer, Hans-Georg. 1976. *Philosophical Hermeneutics.* Translated and edited by David E. Linge. Berkeley: University of California Press.

———. 2004. *Truth and Method.* Translated by Donald G. Marshall and Joel Weinsheimer. New York: Continuum.

Hassan, Zaid. 2014. *The Social Labs Revolution: A New Approach to Solving Our Most Complex Challenges*. San Francisco, CA: Berrett-Koehler Publishers.

Hoerr, John. 1988. *And the Wolf Finally Came: The Decline and Fall of the American Steel Industry*. Pittsburgh, PA: University of Pittsburgh Press.

Kapitzke, Cushla. 1995. *Literacy and Religion: The Textual Politics and Practice of Seventh-Day Adventism*. Studies in Written Language and Literacy. Philadelphia, PA: John Benjamins Publishing Company.

Karolak, Hannah, and Craig T. Maier. 2015. "From 'Safe Spaces' to 'Communicative Spaces': Semiotic Labor, Authentic Civility, and the Basic Communication Course." *Journal of the Association for Communication Administration* 34, no. 2: 88–101.

Kauhanen-Simanainen, Anne. 2007. *Corporate Literacy: Discovering the Senses of the Organisation*. Oxford: Chandos Publishing.

Keay, Douglas. 1987. "Interview with Margaret Thatcher." *Woman's Own*, September 23, 1987.

Keith, William. 2007. *Democracy as Discussion: The American Forum Movement and Adult Civic Education*. Lanham, MD: Lexington Books.

Klinenberg, Eric. 2018. *Palaces for the People: How Social Infrastructure Can Help Fight Inequality, Polarization, and the Decline of Civic Life*. New York: Crown.

Lipari, Lisbeth. 2014. *Listening, Thinking, Being: Toward an Ethics of Attunement*. University Park: The Pennsylvania State University Press.

Lippmann, Walter. 1993. *The Phantom Public*. New Brunswick, NJ: Transaction Publishers.

MacIntyre, Alasdair. 2007. *After Virtue: A Study in Moral Theory*. 3rd ed. South Bend, IN: University of Notre Dame Press.

Maier, Craig T. 2018. "Light and Shadows: Appreciative Inquiry, Communication Ethics Literacy, and the Opioid Epidemic." *Qualitative Research Reports in Communication* 19, no. 1: 62–67. https://doi.org/10.1080/17459435.2018.1529699.

McLean, Katherine. 2016. ""There's Nothing Here": Deindustrialization as Risk Environment for Overdose." *International Journal of Drug Policy* 29: 19–26. https://doi.org/10.1016/j.drugpo.2016.01.009.

McNamara, Patrick J. 2007. *Sons of the Sierra: Juárez, Díaz, and the People of Ixtlán, Oaxaca, 1855–1920*. Chapel Hill: University of North Carolina Press.

Peters, John D. 1999. *Speaking into the Air: A History of the Idea of Communication*. Chicago, IL: University of Chicago Press.

Phillips, Derek L. 1993. *Looking Backward: A Critical Appraisal of Communitarian Thought*. Princeton, NJ: Princeton University Press.

Putnam, Robert. 2000. *Bowling Alone: The Collapse and Revival of American Community*. New York: Simon & Schuster.

Rorty, Richard. 1979. *Philosophy and the Mirror of Nature*. Princeton, NJ: Princeton University Press.

Ross, Andrew. 2009. *Nice Work If You Can Get It: Life and Labor in Precarious Times.* New York: New York University Press.

Sennett, Richard. 1998. *The Corrosion of Character.* New York: W. W. Norton & Company.

———. 2006. *The Culture of the New Capitalism.* New Haven, CT: Yale University Press.

Seward, Dan E. 2019. "Orchestrated Online Conversation: Designing Asynchronous Discussion Boards for Interactive, Incremental, and Communal Literacy Development in First-Year College Writing." *Research in Online Literacy Education* 1, no. 1. http://www.roleolor.org/seward-orchestrated-online-conversation.html.

Standing, Guy. 2014. *The Precariat: The New Dangerous Class.* London: Bloomsbury.

Taylor, Charles. 1992. *Sources of the Self.* Cambridge, MA: Harvard University Press.

van der Kolk, Bessel. 2014. *The Body Keeps the Score: Brain, Mind, and Body in the Healing of Trauma.* New York: Penguin.

Vandi, Loretta. 2015. "The Visual Vernacular: The Construction of Communal Literacy at the Convent of Santa Maria in Pontetetto (Lucca)." In *Nuns' Literacies in Medieval Europe: The Kansas City Dialogue*, edited by Virginia Blanton, Veronica O'Mara, and Patricia Stoop, 171–89. Turnhout, Belgium: Brepols Publishers.

Weil, Simone. 1952. *The Need for Roots.* Translated by Arthur F. Wills. New York: Routledge.

Wynter-Hoyte, Kamania, and Gloria S. Boutte. 2018. "Expanding Understandings of Literacy: The Double Consciousness of a Black Middle Class Child in Church and School." *The Journal of Negro Education* 87, no. 4: 375–90. https://doi.org/10.7709/jnegroeducation.87.4.0375.

Zoorob, Michael J., and Jason L. Salemi. 2017. "Bowling Alone, Dying Together: The Role of Social Capital in Mitigating the Drug Overdose Epidemic in the United States." *Drug and Alcohol Dependence* 173: 1–9. https://doi.org/10.1016/j.drugalcdep.2016.12.011.

3 Framing Participatory Community Inquiry (PCI)

The notion of "communal literacy" suggests a pedagogy of some kind. But what kind of pedagogy is best suited to communal literacy? The Brazilian critical educator Paulo Freire (2000) argued that the traditional understanding of literacy, which sees learning as a technical process in which students are force-fed prepackaged lessons while sitting in orderly rows in a classroom, ultimately alienates students—especially students from marginalized backgrounds—because it does not speak to the realities of their everyday lives. Instead, he argued, we need to see literacy as emerging from an open-ended, learner-centered experience that helps people become conscious of and speak to the challenges they face. Learning to read and write about their daily lives allows people, especially people living under various forms of oppression, to give voice to what matters most to them in ways that can transform society for the better.

Freire's (2000) approach resonates strongly with what is called action research, a methodology originated by psychologist Kurt Lewin (1946) in the 1940s as a social intervention for improving race relations. Based on the belief that communities already possess the wisdom they need to respond to their challenges, action research has come to represent a diverse array of ways for helping community members understand and transform their lives together. Despite this diversity, Stephen Kemmis, Robin McTaggart, and Rhonda Nixon (2014) observe that action research projects all share a commitment to (1) affirming the role of participants as co-inquirers in the learning process and (2) shaping the research to enable the participants themselves to improve their communities and lives. As Orlando Fals-Borda (1991) remarks, these commitments make action research simultaneously a form of inquiry, a form of adult education, and a theory of social action intended to generate political and social transformation.

DOI: 10.4324/9781003243663-4

This chapter explores how Participatory Community Inquiry (PCI) incorporates the principles of action research to foster communal literacy. Instead of assuming that community members are communally illiterate—and immediately jumping to programs of remedial education that would serve only to humiliate and alienate them—it aims to help community members acknowledge, understand, and deepen the values that *already* drive their lives together, with the confidence that those beliefs are strong enough to help them reply to the challenges they face. In other words, PCI facilitates an "offering up" rather than a "preaching down." As it does so, PCI allows community members to answer fundamental questions that correspond to the three dimensions of communal literacy—attending to what matters, being present to each other, and caring for the common: *What do we value most? How can we acknowledge and respect those things in our everyday communication with each other? How can we take actions that care for the places and spaces that allow us to flourish?*

PCI strives to answer these questions with an approach that is (1) appreciative in intent, (2) practice-driven, and (3) action-oriented— elements that also correspond to the facets of communal literacy. This approach may be used with inquiry groups that reflect various mixtures of homogeneity or heterogeneity, depending on the overall intent of the study. As Pranee Liamputtong (2011) observes, homogeneous groups, in which participants share a particular set of experiences and backgrounds, can be helpful when working with segments of a community who have been marginalized and require a greater sense of safety in order to talk freely, while heterogeneous groups drawn from a broad cross-section of the community can be important in raising a diversity of perspectives and views. Within the context of PCI, inquiry groups will be homogeneous in the sense that participants will have a shared history that comes from living within the community. But because communal literacy requires people to engage with others who are different than they are, PCI requires some level of heterogeneity, as well. This heterogeneity can most obviously come through racial, ethnic, and gender diversity. However, in communities like Southton where racial diversity is low, diversity in social class, professional expertise, political affiliation, religious background, or life experience can be just as important.

Appreciative in Intent

Today, discussions of community take place amidst constant cynicism, institutional distrust, political polarization, economic anxieties, depression over climate change, and deep frustration and anger over systemic racism, sexism, and classism. All of these factors have been amplified by the coronavirus pandemic. However, while these emotions are all too often as legitimate as they are deeply felt, these feelings are not a good place to begin conversations designed to bring people together and facilitate social learning. In their groundbreaking essay on groups in crisis, Frank J. Barrett and David L. Cooperrider (1990) argue that beginning with expressions of negative emotions like fear, anger, and cynicism quickly generates a paralyzing, vicious cycle of grievance-airing and defensiveness. As a result, instead of focusing on the problems that groups face, they advocate beginning with a different set of questions that encourage members to create values that unite them, reinterpret the past in constructive ways, accept responsibility for their lives together, and develop a compelling sense of purpose that can help them move into the future.

Testing this hypothesis in a deeply divided organization, Barrett and Cooperrider (1990) found that teams of inquirers who focused on the strengths they saw and the future they desired to create generated better solutions than those engaged in more traditional types of problem-focused problem-solving. Engaging social problems with an appreciative intent, they argue, generated a constructive critical consciousness that liberated people to think in new ways. "Appreciation is a poetic process that fosters a fresh perception of ordinary life," they write. "Unlike the evaluating stance of problem-solving, which is based on the assumption of deficiency, appreciation refers to an affirmative valuing of experience based on belief, trust, and conviction" (1990, 236). This alternative approach, which Cooperrider would come to call *appreciative inquiry*, contends that acknowledging an organization's strengths is a foundation for articulating its aspirations for the future and designing ways to bring that positive vision to reality.

Writing with Suresh Srivastva, Cooperrider (Cooperrider and Srivastva 2001) frames appreciative inquiry as a branch of action research that is deliberately *appreciative*, *applicable*, *provocative*, and *collaborative* in approach. Instead of beginning with problems, it seeks strengths, contending that aligning strengths is the best way to overcome perceived weaknesses. Instead of producing disembodied "facts," it seeks generative knowledge that organization members can use. Instead of promoting neutral detachment, it seeks to promote active engagement, compelling visions, and stronger commitment. Instead of relegating the research process to leaders or consultants alone, it involves all of the members of a social system in the search for solutions. And instead of beginning from a place of scientific detachment, it embraces a reverence and wonder at human life together. As a form of social learning and intervention, appreciative inquiry aims to foster what J. Kevin Barge and Christine Oliver (2003) call the *affirmative competence* to recognize strengths within a social system, the *expansive competence* to promote new ways of thinking about the issues the system faces, the *generative competence* to invite and nurture growth and change, and the *collaborative competence* to develop relationships in a diverse world.

In this respect, appreciative inquiry and the social learning it strives to promote resonate with the work of Arnett, Fritz, and McManus (2018), who similarly emphasize the importance of paying attention to "goods" that a community needs to protect and promote: the highest values that they strive to uphold, the strengths that they believe they still have to offer, the norms and institutions that give a positive shape to their lives, and the aspirations and hopes that motivate them to change. As mentioned in the previous chapter, stories and goods are closely related, with goods crystalizing the values stories hold into touchstones for community life. The extraordinary cultural and social diversity of contemporary society means that communities will be awash in stories intersecting and interacting with each other. Even though each of these accounts is worth our attention, their diversity often makes it difficult to achieve agreement on the level of story. But because people can value the same thing for different reasons—as we saw with the Quaker and the Marine in the previous chapter—achieving agreement on goods, while more modest, is more achievable. For this reason, PCI employs various forms of story work (Kurtz 2014) but focuses this activity on surfacing and clarifying social goods to create a set of minimal values (Bok 2002) that begin the conversation on a concrete and generative footing.

In doing so, PCI seeks to begin with what Cooperrider would see as an *appreciative intent*. Beginning with an appreciative intent does not mean that PCI dwells in a fantasy world where "bads" do not exist or are unimportant for a community's life together, that it delegitimizes questioning or challenging the status quo, or that it dodges painful truths in order to cater to the "fragility" of dominant groups (DiAngelo 2018). Appreciative intent is grounded in decades of research in positive psychology by the likes of scholars like Barbara L. Fredrickson (1998, 2001, 2009), whose *broaden-and-build model* of positive emotions suggests that while negative emotions like anger, frustration, and fear are vital in making people aware of dangers in their environment, positive emotions like wonder, joy, and curiosity are even more important because they *broaden* people's awareness of possible solutions to those problems and help them *build* the resources they need to respond to the challenges they face.

Fredrickson (1998, 2001, 2009) does not advocate banishing negative emotions, but rather balancing them with positive ones. Indeed, she argues that achieving the proper ratio—about three positive emotions for every negative one—opens the door to a number of compelling outcomes, in which people see the world and each other differently. For example, Fredrickson (2009) cites research showing that those steeped in positive emotions are actually far more able to recognize the unique facial features in people of other races, while those locked in negative mindsets tend to see members of other races as looking all the same. "Positive emotions didn't simply diminish entrenched racial bias, it eliminated it altogether," she writes. "Under the influence of positivity, people became just as good at recognizing individuals of another race as they are at recognizing individuals of their own race" (2009, 68). In this way, appreciative intent is a strategic move with profound ethical importance, expanding people's problem-solving capacity and their ability—literally, it seems—to see the face of the Other.

Fredrickson's (2001) broaden-and-build model connects to Carol S. Dweck's (2007) work on mindsets. Dweck distinguishes between *fixed mindsets* and *growth mindsets*. Persons with fixed mindsets, she argues, assume that their attributes and abilities are more or less unchanging, while those with growth mindsets consider themselves constant works in progress. Those who believe their capabilities and resources to be fixed, Dweck continues, encounter setbacks as permanent failures, are less likely to commit to learning and improving themselves, and see themselves as living in a constricted world continually under threat. The opposite is true for those who possess growth mindsets. Although Dweck's work focuses primarily on individual cognition and motivation, differences in mindset can have important implications for leadership and group problem-solving, either constricting thinking to pre-ordained, "safe" options or allowing for creative inquiry and learning. Taken together, Dweck's and Fredrickson's research suggests how appreciative approaches can help individuals and groups shift from one mindset to another. Their work proposes that when grounded in goods that inspire them and connect them to what they value most, people will tend to adopt theories of leadership and change that foster collaboration, creativity, and growth. This insight is particularly important for communities facing change and adversity: Those steeped in negativity will gravitate toward static mindsets that crumble under pressure, while those steeped in appreciation may move more easily toward resilience.

Drawing on their own research, Cooperrider and Barrett (2002) make a similar point. The questions people ask, they contend, are decisive in creating the space in which their inquiry unfolds. Inquiries rooted in questions grounded in a negative frame—*How are we being hurt? What have we lost? What do we fear? Who enrages us?*—generate one particular type of solution, while inquiries grounded in appreciation—*Who do we aspire to be? Who can we grow? What gives us hope? Whom do we love?*—open a different repertoire of responses to include approaches that allow people to learn and grow together. To be sure, depending on the situation, either line of questioning may be appropriate. There are times when people absolutely need to speak about their hurts, losses, fears, and anger because these emotions help them surface and acknowledge goods that have long been ignored or are under threat. (In this sense, we might say they are coming to appreciation through the back door.) But when it comes to the practice of protecting and promoting those goods (Arnett, Fritz, and McManus 2018), appreciative inquiry contends that they need to draw from a much broader emotional and relational palette.

Operating from an appreciative intent allows groups to tap these resources. Cooperrider and Barrett (2002) see this insight as opening the spiritual heart of the human sciences. "Inquiry," they conclude, "is the experience of mystery that changes our life" (2000, 59). And the life-changing inquiry Cooperrider and Barrett describe comes not from learning how to develop ever more detailed lists of all the ways a community is failing—a list that will never be finished—but from learning to appreciate how this community, given the myriad imperfections, injustices, and challenges that beset its people, even exists at all. In the process, the principle of appreciative intent fosters communal literacy by encouraging people to look differently at their lives together and, with new eyes, begin to recognize the things that are worth sustaining, defending, nourishing, and giving to others. And this is the mystery Cooperrider and Barrett describe: No matter the difficulties a community faces, no matter how marginalized its people, it always has something to sustain, defend, nourish, and give. As they learn to see these goods at work in their communities, community members embark on a process of social learning that increases their capacity to attend to and wonder about their lives together. This sense of wonder leads to the study's first research question:

RQ1: What are the social goods that give this community life?

Practice-Driven

Cooperrider (2001) contends that social systems are *heliotropic*, constantly tending toward the light, as long as a sufficient amount of appreciative energy is released. Nevertheless, while appreciating the social goods that animate a community is a vital first step, critics of appreciative inquiry have worried that simply focusing on goods alone cannot overcome deep structural problems in social systems (Bushe and Coetzer 1995; Sekerka et al. 2006; Bushe 2007, 2011; Fitzgerald, Oliver, and Hoxsey 2010; Maier 2018). Stephen P. Fitzgerald, Christine Oliver, and Joan C. Hoxsey (2010) in particular observe that looking to the light, in and of itself, is insufficient. Social systems must also attend to the "shadows"—areas of weakness or shame that lie unspoken, unacknowledged assumptions or patterns of behavior that undermine the positive image they want to present to the world, or hidden dynamics of power and marginalization—that obscure or threaten the goods they want to protect and promote (Arnett, Fritz, and McManus 2018). In other words, simply acknowledging social goods is not enough. If community members do not or cannot support these goods in their daily lives, any talk about what matters will be empty.

Indeed, the initial study of Southton and the surrounding communities (Maier 2018) noticed that while respondents more or less easily coalesced around three social goods they wanted to advance—a common belief in the value of *wellness* supported by a commitment to a *continuum of care* and a strong supply of *social capital* within the community—several shadows were looming above them. In their interviews, respondents showed that they understood wellness in different, even incommensurable ways; some reported deep feelings of alienation from the group that, if left unaddressed, would affect the continuum of care; and many described a deeply toxic relational environment that put the strength of the area's social capital in question. Organizational psychologists Chris Argyris and Donald A. Schön (1974) might have described these tensions as gaps between what respondents said they valued (what they would perhaps have called the respondents' *espoused goods*) and the values the respondents' behaviors actually supported (what could be called the respondents' *goods-in-use*). Emphasizing espoused goods without addressing the tensions between these goods and the community's goods-in-use could very well set the stage for cynicism and failure. Still, the study suggested that the presence of these shadows did not necessarily mean that an appreciative intent was unfounded. "Acknowledging such shadows . . . does not mean that AI [appreciative inquiry] is naïve, nor does it mean a return to the preoccupation with 'bads' that AI strives to avoid," the study argued. "Rather, shadows can apply a 'chiaroscuro effect' to AI interventions, sharpening engagement and problem-solving" (Maier 2018, 65). The presence of these shadows suggested a need for a different approach that balanced positive intent with the cultivation of purposeful behaviors that connect social goods to everyday life. Arnett, Fritz, and McManus (2018), following both Alasdair MacIntyre (2007) and Aristotle (1999), call these behaviors *practices.*

Aristotle (1999) roots human flourishing in what he describes as virtuous habits, things we do that, over time, train us to follow the good as if it were second nature to us. In the simplest sense, then, a practice within the context of PCI is an intentional habit that, through repetition, teaches people to do the right thing. As they strengthen something that is going well, improve something that has the potential to grow, or help people avoid things that hold them back, virtuous habits offer a way to put people's money where their mouth is. For MacIntyre (2007), practices bring us into relationship not only with the particular good we desire to advance but also with others who are in the position of telling us whether or not we are living up to the standards and commitments we set for ourselves. And that is the rub of Aristotle's and MacIntyre's understanding of practice: If the practice is good enough, and the social good worthy enough, we never get it perfectly right. As Aristotle observes, the ethical life is like archery, in which repeated attempts may help us get the arrow closer to the bullseye but will never put it precisely in the middle. And for MacIntyre, who sees the building of community as giving rise to a particularly important set of practices, this means that community is not a singular accomplishment that can be done once and then forgotten or a mouldering set of principles put up on some moss-covered stone tablets in the town square. Community takes practice, and if we take our lives together seriously, we should always be practicing it.

The practice of community is humble labor. While naming and acknowledging social goods may make us feel good, living them often requires us to do things that are uncomfortable and earn neither praise nor applause. Moreover, the results of practices may never be readily apparent to those engaged in them. This calls to mind the work of the French spiritual philosopher Simone Weil (1997), who understood the practice of community as a form of active waiting. "The weeds are pulled up by the muscular effort of the peasant," she writes, "but only sun and water can make the corn grow" (1997, 193). Echoing Cooperrider and Barrett's (2002) call to recognize the mystery of social life, Weil emphasizes that the practices that nurture the social goods that truly nourish a community—the sociological equivalents of pulling weeds, watering the plants, or spreading manure—do not create community of their own accord. Community is derivative, a byproduct of its practice that can only be invited into being and never demanded (Maier 2013). What is more, practices are often the most powerful when they are simple, quiet, and unobtrusive, focused on the good being sustained, not the person doing the sustaining. As Janie M. Harden Fritz writes (2013), some of the most powerful things we can do to promote our lives together are *micropractices*, small acts of consideration and kindness like greeting strangers on the street, taking care not to talk over others, or simply showing up and participating in community events—things that seem insignificant but, over time, build into something more.

Within the context of action research, Kemmis, McTaggart, and Nixon (2014) describe practices as things we do, say, or relate to each other in ways that help us live purposeful lives together. Although Kemmis and his colleagues are not communication scholars, their understanding of the practices that action research creates is intrinsically communicative, making it important for the current study. Even practices that seem focused on "doing" instead of "saying" and "relating" can be understood as nonverbal "statements" that sustain a community's communication ecology (Gehrke 2018; Lerner and Gehrke 2018) and, in turn, shape the quality of the conversations that occur among its members. Picking up litter, for instance, advocates for a set of values as it keeps the streets clean, and keeping a weekly calendar of community events on one's desk or cell phone can remind people when, where, and how they need to be present for each other.

What makes a good practice? Practices, Kemmis and his colleagues (2014) argue, should be meaningful to those engaged in them, make sense within the routines and roles of everyday life, and fit the historical moment in which they unfold. But most important, they continue, a good practice encourages those engaged in it to be mindful of their community's values and to recognize how their individual lives connect to their life together. Practices are powerful, Kemmis, McTaggart, and Nixon conclude, because they tie together beliefs about the way the world should be with the ambiguous realities of day-to-day life. In the process, they help community members ensure that the social goods they espouse are the ones they truly put to use (Argyris and Schön 1974).

As they grow into habits of being and acting, practices create a web of meaning that, in the terminology of Weil (1952), gives people's lives together a sense of rootedness. But Kemmis and his co-authors (2014) contend that practices may also need to change when they are no longer appropriate, or new practices may need to be added as times change. For instance, the practice of shaking hands as a form of communicating respect is no longer appropriate in a time of pandemic-related social distancing, but the need to communicate respect for others remains. In reflecting on this practice, we might discover that shaking hands is merely a Western tradition and that there are other ways of communicating respect, such as bowing or other gestures, that people from all cultures can find meaningful and agreeable. This process of talking about, defining, and re-defining practices is an essential form of social learning that challenges people to reflect upon and apply the social goods the practices sustain, instead of clinging to practices that may be inappropriate for the moment.

Although small, when repeated over time by enough people, micropractices like bowing or shaking hands—or, in the case of the coronavirus pandemic, wearing face masks in public places—that are undertaken in support of social goods fundamentally transform not only how groups function but also how the members of the group understand themselves. As MacIntyre (2007) contends, by practicing community we slowly become people capable of living in community. Or to put it differently, we can say that communal literacy grows through living the micropractices of attending to what matters, being present, and caring for the common centers that make a community what it is. In the practice of PCI, this means looking for and designing practices that encourage people to pay attention to the goods, people, and situations around them, show up for others and the community when the situation demands, and look after the things that people hold in common with each other. With that in mind, the current study seeks to understand practice-making through the following research question:

> *RQ2:* What *practices* can help community members live out the social goods that matter most and foster the communal literacy they need for the community to flourish?

Action-Oriented

Kemmis, McTaggart, and Nixon (2014) argue that people engaged in action-oriented inquiry must also know how to situate the practices they design as a part of a broader program of systematic change, what Arnett, Fritz, and McManus (2018) describe as a story that offers people a reason *why* practices matter. Writing on the German political thinker Hannah Arendt (1998), Arnett (2013) suggests that these stories emerge from actions that respond to the challenges the community faces and hold the potential of marking a new beginning in the community's life together. But action is a moment of great risk, as well as an occasion of potential rebirth. As Arendt remarks, the true results of an action are always invisible to those engaged in it. We do not know if we will succeed or fail, or if our good intentions will have unwelcome consequences. Where PCI's appreciative intent focuses on positive problem-solving, and where the process of practice-making encourages people to reflect and make changes in their everyday lives as individuals, action is a risk that the inertia of life all too often discourages people from taking. But action is essential for community vitality. If a community is a conversation about a story that matters, actions mark turning points in that conversation where a community's story can be reinterpreted, retold, or renewed. Without action, the conversation falters, the story grows cold, and the community withers.

Also drawing from Arendt, Argyris (1993) describes how taking action is vital for group learning and growth. Action, he argues, is much more than implementing a plan. Bringing what they know (or think they know) into conversation with what they are doing, action allows community members to test their assumptions about the social goods that sustain their community and the practices that nourish those goods. Trying, failing, and trying again exposes gaps in thinking and knowledge, brings new issues to light, and reveals the resources members need to develop if they are to move forward. Similarly, Kemmis and his colleagues (2014) frame action research as inherently reflective, occurring in an iterative spiral of *planning* change, *acting* out the plan and *observing* the results of that change, *reflecting* on those results, and *re-planning* based on that learning, which in turn begins a new cycle of action, observation, and reflection. In this sense, both Argyris and Kemmis and his co-authors underscore an essential point that Arendt (1998) believes that contemporary society has forgotten: Action and reflection are not opposed but must work together and inform each other. They meet through the act of storytelling that embeds what we do in larger plots that give our experience texture and meaning. In this sense, we can see Kemmis, McTaggart, and Nixon's (2014) action research framework itself as an unending story of planning, experimentation, learning, and growth.

In action, then, PCI completes the circle, returning to the stories that give rise to both the community and the goods that define its life together. Depending on the approach that we are taking, we can frame the story of action research as a search for potential solutions to complex challenges (Hassan 2014), the discovery of new responses to changing environments (Whitney and Trosten-Bloom 2010), or an effort to enact deep societal change (Kemmis, McTaggart, and Nixon 2014). However, Alice McIntyre (2008) reminds us that, regardless of the approach they take, action researchers always see the inquirers as the agents of change. Action research, she argues, is always done *by* those engaged in it and never *to* or *for* them. Or to put it differently, the inquirers, not the researchers, must always be the heroes of the story. For this reason, PCI focuses on actions community members want to take, instead of actions policy makers or experts might take on behalf of the community. Although these external initiatives may be absolutely necessary, especially in under-resourced communities, focusing outward for solutions does little to strengthen the capacity of community members to declare what they need and take ownership of their future. Without this sense of agency and control, community members can see well-meaning initiatives like needle exchange vans or even the social infrastructure investments Eric Klinenberg (2018) champions as disrespectful or even harmful intrusions. As Zaid Hassan (2014) suggests, enabling communities to become active partners instead of passive recipients not only makes for better policies but also guards against community resistance that can undermine potentially essential efforts.

Within the context of PCI, actions focus on responses aimed at strengthening the community's sense of social connection and communication. Kemmis and his colleagues (2014), who are deeply influenced by the work of Jürgen Habermas (1971), emphasize action's role in advancing *emancipatory interests*, in which communities speak truth to power and critique the systematic distortions around them. But while PCI certainly recognizes the importance of engaging communities in crisis with an emancipatory intent, its focus on social goods and community values means that it tends to privilege actions that Habermas would see as promoting a *practical or ethical interest*. Building on Putnam's (2000) model of social capital, we can describe these actions as falling into two broad categories: *bonding actions* and *bridging actions*. Bonding actions focus on strengthening the in-group ties Putnam associates with bonding social capital. These actions can work on a number of levels, depending on the groups that need strengthening. Initiatives to improve how families communicate, for instance, would belong to this category. So would efforts to help members of marginalized communities connect with each other, such as projects designed to bring people with opioid use disorder together to reduce their loneliness, improve their social support, and help them find the resources they need. And so would building community gardens and green spaces that allow residents to rest and provide for each other. Grounded in sameness and homogeneity, bonding actions are foundational efforts, designed to strengthen what Putnam (2000, 23) calls the "sociological superglue" that holds the community together.

While bonding actions strengthen social connections grounded in sameness, bridging actions, in contrast, look outward, strengthening connections across lines of difference. In the process, they create the weak social ties that Putnam (2000) sees as essential in linking people to resources that no single in-group can provide on its own. "Strong ties with intimate friends may ensure chicken soup when you're sick," he writes, "but weak ties with distant acquaintances are more likely to produce leads for a new job" (2000, 363). Bridging actions would most certainly include interracial, intercultural, and interreligious dialogues. They would also include programs to improve communication between police and marginalized communities, as well as initiatives to reduce the stigmatization of people with opioid use disorder. They might also include efforts to advocate for resources or communicate the community's pride to others.

The relationship between bonding and bridging actions is complex. Putnam (2000) makes it clear that both types of social capital are necessary, and there may be situations where a community might realize it needs to build one type of social capital before focusing on the other—or that they need to build both at the same time. Indeed, a single initiative may be a bonding action and a bridging action simultaneously: An initiative to bring the community together to address litter or raise money to repair sidewalks, for instance, may simultaneously offer opportunities for community bonding and serve as bridges that allow the community to demonstrate to others that it is a safe, beautiful place to live. "Bonding and bridging are not 'either-or' categories into which social networks can be evenly divided," Putnam (2000, 23) writes, "but 'more or less' dimensions along which we can compare different forms of social capital." Bonding actions are absolutely necessary, but they must be balanced with bridging actions designed to balance what Putnam sees as bonding social capital's dark side. Finding the right mix can be difficult. Here, the task involves finding which types of bonds to support, but discovering what those bonds are and how to strengthen them takes time, practice, and care. For this reason, PCI's commitment to action must be understood as a commitment to reflection and learning, an ongoing story of a heroic search for what works.

As Hassan (2014) observes, action planning works best when actions are seen as prototypes or experiments instead of polished initiatives. Instead of focusing on one or two actions, he contends, groups need to focus on developing a portfolio of proposals, with the assumption that some may work while others fizzle. The action phase, then, is ultimately as much a part of the inquiry process as the other two elements. By designing and undertaking actions to support social connection, community members can learn more about the social goods that animate them and the practices that sustain those goods. They may learn, for instance, that they need to think differently about a particular social good or that a social good they thought was vital may not be as important as they initially thought. They may discover that the practices developed to foster those goods may themselves require a greater level of community-level support and engagement than initially supposed. In the process, they can discover how communal literacy grows through learning what it really takes to bond and bridge the community together. Undertaking actions helps them understand where the needs are, where power truly resides, how the community actually works, and what needs to happen to keep the conversation going (Rorty 1979). The need to encourage this learning leads to the study's third question:

RQ3: How can residents generate *actions* that bond and bridge a community together?

Through these three questions, PCI creates a circle of social learning that encourages the development of communal literacy. Acknowledging and appreciating the social goods that give the community life fosters communal literacy by reminding community members of what they share and showing them that regardless of what has happened to them and the uncertainties they face, there is still something in their lives together worth protecting and promoting (Arnett, Fritz, and McManus 2018). Designing and engaging in practices that intentionally nurture those social goods builds communal literacy by encouraging community members to put their money where their mouth is and, over time, allow those social goods to shape them, as well. Finally, undertaking actions that strengthen bonds and build bridges within and across groups cultivates communal literacy by teaching people what life together truly demands and by inviting stories that encourage them to see their community anew. To see how this process could work, a five-week pilot project was conducted in Southton that explored how two inquiry groups of residents encountered PCI and the social learning that occurred. The next chapter describes the methodology that guided the effort.

References

Arendt, Hannah. 1998. *The Human Condition*. 2nd ed. Chicago, IL: University of Chicago Press.

Argyris, Chris. 1993. *Knowledge for Action: A Guide to Overcoming Barriers to Organizational Change*. San Francisco, CA: Jossey-Bass.

Argyris, Chris, and Donald Schön. 1974. *Theory in Practice: Increasing Professional Effectiveness*. San Francisco, CA: Jossey-Bass.

Aristotle. 1999. *Nicomachean Ethics*. 2nd ed. Translated by Terence Irwin. Indianapolis, IN: Hackett Publishing Company.

Arnett, Ronald C. 2013. *Communication Ethics in Dark Times: Hannah Arendt's Rhetoric of Warning and Hope*. Carbondale: Southern Illinois University Press.

Arnett, Ronald C., Janie M. Harden Fritz, and Leeanne M. Bell McManus. 2018. *Communication Ethics Literacy: Dialogue and Difference*. 2nd ed. Dubuque, IA: Kendall Hunt Publishing.

Barge, J. Kevin, and Christine Oliver. 2003. "Working with Appreciation in Managerial Practice." *Academy of Management Review* 28, no. 1: 124–42. https://doi.org/10.5465/amr.2003.8925244.

Barrett, Frank J., and David L. Cooperrider. 1990. "Generative Metaphor Intervention: A New Approach for Working with Systems Divided by Conflict and Caught in Defensive Perception." *The Journal of Applied Behavioral Science* 26, no. 2: 236. https://doi.org/10.1177/0021886390262011.

Bok, Sissela. 2002. *Common Values*. Columbia: University of Missouri Press.

Bushe, Gervase R. 2007. "Appreciative Inquiry is Not (Just) About the Positive." *OD Practitioner* 39, no. 4: 30–35.

———. 2011. "Appreciative Inquiry: Theory and Critique." In *The Routledge Companion to Organizational Change*, edited by David Boje, Bernard Burnes, and John Hassard, 87–103. Oxford: Routledge.

Bushe, Gervase R., and Grahme Coetzer. 1995. "Appreciative Inquiry as a Team-Development Intervention: A Controlled Experiment." *The Journal of Applied Behavioral Science* 31, no. 1: 13–30. https://doi.org/10.1177/0021886395311004.

Cooperrider, David L. 2001. "Positive Image, Positive Action: The Affirmative Basis of Organizing." In *Appreciative Inquiry: An Emerging Direction for Organization Development*, edited by David Cooperrider, Peter F. Sorensen Jr., Therese F. Yeager, and Diana Whitney, 31–76. Champaign, IL: Stipes.

Cooperrider, David L., and Frank J. Barrett. 2002. "An Exploration of the Spiritual Heart of Human Science Inquiry." *Reflections: The SoL Journal* 3, no. 3: 56–62. https://doi.org/10.1162/152417302317363921.

Cooperrider, David L. and Suresh Srivastva. 2001. "Appreciative Inquiry in Organizational Life." In *Appreciative Inquiry: An Emerging Direction for Organization Development*, edited by David Cooperrider, Peter F. Sorensen Jr., Therese F. Yeager, and Diana Whitney, 77–100. Champaign, IL: Stipes.

DiAngelo, Robin. 2018. *White Fragility*. Boston, MA: Beacon Press.

Dweck, Carol S. 2007. *Mindset: The New Psychology of Success*. New York: Ballantine.

Fals-Borda, Orlando. 1991. "Some Basic Ingredients." In *Action and Knowledge: Breaking the Monopoly with Participatory Action Research*, edited by Orlando Fals-Borda and Muhammad Anisur Rahman, 3–12. New York: The Apex Press.

Fitzgerald, Stephen P., Christine Oliver, and Joan C. Hoxsey. 2010. "Appreciative Inquiry as a Shadow Process," *Journal of Management Inquiry* 19, no. 3: 220–33, https://doi.org/10.1177/1056492609349349.

Fredrickson, Barbara L. 1998. "What Good Are Positive Emotions?" *Review of General Psychology* 2, no. 3: 300–19. https://doi.org/10.1037/1089-2680.2.3.300.

———. 2001. "The Role of Positive Emotions in Positive Psychology: The Broaden-and-Build Theory of Positive Emotions." *American Psychologist* 56, no. 3: 218–26. https://doi.org/10.1037/0003-066x.56.3.218.

———. 2009. *Positivity*. New York: Crown.

Freire, Paulo. 2000. *Pedagogy of the Oppressed*. 30th anniversary ed. New York: Continuum.

Fritz, Janie M. Harden. 2013. *Professional Civility: Communicative Virtue at Work*. New York: Peter Lang.

Gehrke, Pat J. 2018. *Nano-Publics: Communicating Nanotechnology Applications, Risks, and Regulations*. New York: Springer International Publishing.

Habermas, Jürgen. 1971. *Knowledge and Human Interests*. Translated by Jeremy J. Shapiro. Boston: Beacon Press.

Hassan, Zaid. 2014. *The Social Labs Revolution: A New Approach to Solving Our Most Complex Challenges*. San Francisco, CA: Berrett-Koehler Publishers.

Kemmis, Stephen, Robin McTaggart, and Rhonda Nixon. 2014. *The Action Research Planner: Doing Critical Participatory Action Research*. New York: Springer.

Klinenberg, Eric. 2018. *Palaces for the People: How Social Infrastructure Can Help Fight Inequality, Polarization, and the Decline of Civic Life*. New York: Crown.

Kurtz, Cynthia F. 2014. *Working with Stories in Your Community or Organization: Participatory Narrative Inquiry*. 3rd ed. Northville, NY: Kurtz-Fernhout Publishing.

Lerner, Adam S., and Pat J. Gehrke. 2018. *Organic Public Engagement: How Ecological Thinking Transforms Public Engagement with Science*. New York: Palgrave.

Lewin, Kurt. 1946. "Action Research and Minority Problems." *Journal of Social Issues* 2, no. 4: 34–46. https://doi.org/10.1111/j.1540-4560.1946.tb02295.x.

Liamputtong, Pranee. 2011. *Focus Group Methodology: Principles and Practice.* Thousand Oaks, CA: Sage.

MacIntyre, Alasdair. 2007. *After Virtue: A Study in Moral Theory.* 3rd ed. South Bend, IN: University of Notre Dame Press.

Maier, Craig T. 2013. "Attentive Waiting in an Uprooted Age: Simone Weil's Response in an Age of Precarity." *Review of Communication* 13, no. 3: 225–42. https://doi.org/10.1080/15358593.2013.843715.

———. 2018. "Light and Shadows: Appreciative Inquiry, Communication Ethics Literacy, and the Opioid Epidemic." *Qualitative Research Reports in Communication* 19, no. 1: 62–67. https://doi.org/10.1080/17459435.2018.1529699.

McIntyre, Alice. 2008. *Participatory Action Research.* Qualitative Research Methods Series 52. Thousand Oaks, CA: Sage.

Putnam, Robert. 2000. *Bowling Alone: The Collapse and Revival of American Community.* New York: Simon & Schuster.

Rorty, Richard. 1979. *Philosophy and the Mirror of Nature.* Princeton, NJ: Princeton University Press.

Sekerka, Leslie E., Anne M. Brumbaugh, José Antonio Rosa, and David Cooperrider. 2006. "Comparing Appreciative Inquiry to a Diagnostic Technique in Organizational Change: The Moderating Effects of Gender." *International Journal of Organization Theory & Behavior* 9, no. 4: 449–89. https://doi.org/10.1108/ijotb-09-04-2006-b001.

Weil, Simone. 1952. *The Need for Roots.* Translated by Arthur F. Wills. New York: Routledge.

———. 1997. *Gravity and Grace.* Translated by Arthur Wills. Lincoln: University of Nebraska Press.

Whitney, Diana, and Amanda Trosten-Bloom. 2010. *The Power of Appreciative Inquiry: A Practical Guide to Positive Change.* 2nd ed. San Francisco, CA: Berrett-Koehler.

4   Study Methodology

Ortrun Zuber-Skerritt (1996) notes that action research approaches can take a number of forms ranging from long-term, emancipatory projects that aim at revolutionary social change to more limited endeavors focused on more practical outcomes, such as strategic planning or change management (see also Fals-Borda 1991; McIntyre 2008; Whitney and Trosten-Bloom 2010). Because it focuses on a more or less defined structure and objective, Participatory Community Inquiry (PCI) falls into Zuber-Skerrit's practical line of research. Like appreciative inquiry, which is similarly intentional and structured (see Whitney and Trosten-Bloom 2010), PCI invites participants on a three-step process to surface goods, define practices, and design actions to improve their lives together. Yet, despite this structure, it embraces what Bridget Somekh (2006) sees as the hallmarks of action research: By positioning participants as the inquirers through a process that liberates them to think and create together, PCI aims to facilitate deep learning that can enable participants to effect lasting change in their lives and communities.

This and the following chapter explore how a PCI project might be structured to foster that learning by describing a five-week pilot project in the neighborhood of Southton, located in the southern part of Pittsburgh, Pennsylvania. As discussed in previous chapters, the Southton neighborhood was chosen because it, like the neighborhoods around it, had suffered heavily from the opioid epidemic, and because it was thought that existing relationships between the research team and key stakeholders and community groups would make it easier to conduct the research. One of the lead members of the research team not only was a lifelong Southton resident who had close ties to the neighborhood but was also working as the liaison between the local Pittsburgh City Council member and the community groups, nonprofit organizations, and public safety professionals closest to the opioid epidemic. In particular,

DOI: 10.4324/9781003243663-5

he worked closely with the South Pittsburgh Opioid Action Coalition (SPOAC), an interagency group that brings together voices from throughout the community, including those in recovery from opioid use disorder. The relationship with SPOAC allowed the team to connect to a broad cross-section of community leadership, including city government, businesses and community groups, local nonprofit agencies, religious institutions, schools, public safety officials, and health care providers. These community ties played an essential role in recruitment.

After the initial conception of the study, the research team sought and gained approval from the university's institutional review board in April 2019. Throughout the summer of 2019, the research team worked to recruit participants via its connections with SPOAC and a wide variety of other community groups. The team intended to gather a heterogeneous group of residents representing community members, public safety officials, representatives from law enforcement, business and nonprofit owners, and persons in recovery. Although the team was successful enough to fill two inquiry groups of six and five persons, respectively, recruitment was extraordinarily difficult. These difficulties seemed to have arisen in part because of the length of the project and in part because Southton residents were wary of revisiting a deep community trauma. In addition, persons in recovery seemed particularly reluctant to participate in mixed groups where they did not feel safe enough to share their stories. Yet, the recruitment challenges, even with the support of SPOAC and the research team's liaison's close ties with its member organizations and position within the City Council office, suggest a deeper lack of engagement within the community itself. In other words, the difficulties in attracting participants to the study could in part be evidence of the very problem the study was attempting to address.

The inquiry groups occurred over five 90-minute sessions on successive Wednesday nights in October 2019. Of the eleven participants, six (55 percent) were male and five (45 percent) were female, and ten (91 percent) were white and one (9 percent) was Black. Although the lack of diversity within the groups was a challenge and likely the result of the recruitment problems the research team experienced, the high percentage of white participants did reflect the demographics of the community as a whole, which was 89.7 percent white. After the first session, two of the participants declined to participate in the study. Over the following weeks, not every participant was able to be at every meeting. A rally in Pittsburgh by President Donald Trump in October 2019, for instance, made it impossible for some participants, especially those who worked in public safety and law enforcement, to attend.

Even so, participation was sufficient to enable a substantive and productive discussion throughout the five sessions, and the research team
and facilitators took steps to ensure that those who missed one session
could participate fully in the next.

Over the five weeks, the inquiry groups participated in several exercises exploring the core questions of PCI and were invited, but not required, to engage in inquiry exercises between sessions to deepen their
reflections. Audio recordings of the sessions, as well as the inquiry
exercises, were transcribed for textual analysis, with careful coding
and editing to preserve the anonymity of the participants. Once transcribed, all originals were destroyed, again to preserve anonymity.
A qualitative analysis of the data was conducted to identify the key
themes and metaphors that emerged from the discussion.

The qualitative analysis followed what Barney G. Glaser and Anselm
L. Strauss (1967) call *grounded theory*, an approach uniquely suited to
action research. Within Glaser and Strauss's methodology, theoretical
reflection is understood to emerge from the data itself, unlike quantita-
tive approaches that aim to test predetermined hypotheses. Grounded
theories, they contend, result in research findings that are far more
useful than what Glaser and Strauss call *grand theories*—that is, theories that aim to offer final answers for all times and places—because
grounded theories speak back directly to the unique situations from
which they emerge. "Generating a theory from data means that most
hypotheses and concepts not only come from the data," Glaser and
Strauss (1967, 6) write, "but are systematically worked out in relation
to the data during the course of the research." This process is rigor-
ous but playful, a hermeneutic process of comparative interpretation
that places the part in constant conversation with the whole (Gadamer
2004). Grounded theory thus resonates deeply with PCI, which sees
goods, practices, and actions as rooted within the history and life of a
particular local community (Arnett, Fritz, and McManus 2018).

Glaser and Strauss (1967) describe grounded theory as a process in
which data collection and interpretation coincides with the development of ever more complex and nuanced theories capable of transforming the contexts from which they emerge. In their view, data
collection and coding should be a recursive process of interpretation
leading to the development of hypotheses that serve as the foundation
for developing theories that are as close to the "'real' world" as possible (1967, 42). They write:

> Joint collection, coding, and analysis of data is the underlying
> operation. The generation of theory, coupled with the notion of

theory as process, requires that all three operations be done together as much as possible. They should blur and intertwine continually, from the beginning of an investigation to its end.

(1967, 43)

Following this example, the current study adopted a recursive approach throughout the data collection and analysis. The research team met weekly to connect the data collected to the broader community context. Once the data was transcribed, two members of the research team independently coded the data in light of the team's weekly discussions. These independent analyses were then reconciled to create a single conceptual framework that allowed for a more nuanced understanding of the themes and priorities that emerged from the sessions. This framework was then used to develop a coherent theoretical narrative of the goods, practices, and actions that tells the story of the inquiry groups' development over the five weeks. The following chapter describes the results of this work.

References

Arnett, Ronald C., Janie M. Harden Fritz, and Leeanne M. Bell McManus. 2018. *Communication Ethics Literacy: Dialogue and Difference.* 2nd ed. Dubuque, IA: Kendall Hunt Publishing.

Fals-Borda, Orlando. 1991. "Some Basic Ingredients." In *Action and Knowledge: Breaking the Monopoly with Participatory Action Research*, edited by Orlando Fals-Borda and Muhammad Anisur Rahman, 3–12. New York: The Apex Press.

Gadamer, Hans-Georg. 2004. *Truth and Method.* Translated by Donald G. Marshall and Joel Weinsheimer. New York: Continuum.

Glaser, Barney G., and Anselm L. Strauss. 1967. *The Discovery of Grounded Theory: Strategies for Qualitative Research.* New Brunswick, NJ: AldineTransaction.

McIntyre, Alice. 2008. *Participatory Action Research.* Qualitative Research Methods Series 52. Thousand Oaks, CA: Sage.

Somekh, Bridget. 2006. *Action Research: A Methodology for Change and Development.* New York: Open University Press.

Whitney, Diana, and Amanda Trosten-Bloom. 2010. *The Power of Appreciative Inquiry: A Practical Guide to Positive Change.* 2nd ed. San Francisco, CA: Berrett-Koehler.

Zuber-Skerritt, Ortrun. 1996. "Introduction: New Directions in Action Research." In *New Directions in Action Research*, edited by Ortrun Zuber-Skerritt, 3–7. London: Falmer Press.

5   Results

After a brief introduction to the project and a few bites of pizza, the inquiry groups began their work in the first week of October 2019. Although the discussions were tentative at first, participants took quickly to the project, and the conversations flowed well throughout the five sessions, illustrating how an appreciative intent can encourage participants to consider the social goods that draw them together, design practices to support those goods, and propose actions that can tell new stories capable of transforming the community's life. This chapter will proceed session by session, summarizing each in turn.

Session One: Stories of "Home"

The goal of the first session was to begin to understand the social goods that drew the Southton community together. Building on the premise that goods emerge from stories (Arnett, Fritz, and McManus 2018), the session began with a prompt asking participants to tell a story about a time when they "felt *most* at home in their community." The focus on feeling *most* at home was important since some participants might not have felt the same sense of attachment to Southton as others did. However, in keeping with the overall appreciative intent, this prompt was designed to focus participants' attention on the positive aspects of their community in as much detail as possible. Participants were asked to consider this peak experience deeply: *What happened? Whom were they with? Where were they? How did this experience make them feel "at home"? What did it tell them about what Southton is and can be as a community?* The exercise generated a considerable amount of discussion and energy. Indeed, some participants mentioned later that while they were startled that the study would begin in this way, focusing on positive feelings of home immediately

DOI: 10.4324/9781003243663-6

took their inquiry group's conversation in a constructive direction and avoided the defensiveness and conflict that often coincided with the discussions they were used to having about their community and the opioid epidemic taking place there.

Although there were differences between the groups—Group B focused on the importance of faith in feeling at home, while Group A took a more secular direction—both conversations surfaced similar types of stories: experiencing unexpected kindness when moving into the neighborhood, running into people they know when walking the dog or picking up litter on the street, seeing neighbors helping each other in times of need, feeling safe and known by others, or joining in impromptu neighborhood gatherings. One story, however, summed up what everyone seemed to feel. "I've been here 45 years," said one participant in Group B, who apologized for being of few words. "I just wrote simple. We'd always play football in my backyard, my brothers and sisters, all our neighborhood kids, everybody knew each other, neighbors are more like families, there was always a strong bond between everybody, everyone supported each other." Like this story, many also contained a hint of sadness, as if participants were recounting a world that they knew no longer existed and believed would never exist again.

After writing the stories, each participant read their account aloud to the others, who listened and wrote down anything they believed was positive or good on Post-it Notes, one idea per note. Then, the group quickly clustered the notes into categories. The categories served as a tentative list of social goods (see Table 5.1). The respective lists were subtly different. Group A's list focused on pride, participation, and vigilance to protect and promote community well-being, perhaps because some of the members were in law enforcement. In contrast, Group B's list emphasized the importance of the bonding social capital that comes from faith and close relational ties (Putnam 2000). Despite these subtle differences, the lists were similar in their focus on community activities and traditions that create a sense of social support and neighborliness.

Over the following week, participants tested their respective group's list by looking for and recording three moments when they saw these social goods occurring in their everyday lives. For each instance, they were asked to write a short story reflecting on what happened, how that social good was put into practice, what it meant to the people involved, and what made it reflective of the Southton community as a whole. Participants' responses formed the foundation of the following week's session.

Table 5.1 Initial list of social goods from session one

Group A	Group B
• Accessibility	• Giving Support
• Neighborliness	• Bonding
• Active Participation	• Community Activities
• Livability	• Family Ties
• Community Activities and Assets	• Faith
• Vigilance	• Environment
• Pride and Hope	

Session Two: The Importance of Being "Nebby"

The second session focused on using participants' inquiry activities to help them reinterpret, prioritize, and define the social goods they had developed during the previous week. After reviewing the list, which was displayed on butcher paper for everyone to see, each participant turned to a partner to recount a moment from the previous week they believed reflected the essence of Southton and spoke to one or more of the social goods on the list. When they finished, the roles reversed: The partner had a chance to tell their story, and the initial storyteller had a chance to listen. Participants who were less comfortable with writing than others were simply asked to reflect and tell a story from memory.

Once the stories were exchanged, each participant retold the story that they had heard in their own words to the group. This procedure, called reflective interviewing (Maier and DeIuliis 2015), was deliberate. Having to retell the other person's story in their own words challenged participants to listen more carefully to each other, and hearing their own story as interpreted by another allowed them to see what they said in a new light and called their attention to details that might have been invisible to them at first. After hearing their story retold to them, each storyteller then named the social goods that they heard were present, and a check mark was placed next to each on the butcher paper. Multiple social goods could be present in the same story. Once the group was finished, the respective "votes" were tallied, and the discussion then turned toward narrowing the list of goods to a more concise and manageable list of three or four.

As they narrowed the list, participants could rename or combine elements. In Group A, a particularly interesting conversation focused on the limits of *neighborliness* and *vigilance*—specifically, where they stopped being positive goods to become annoying or even harmful.

To clarify the issue, the participants introduced a bit of Pittsburghese: *nebbiness*. On one level, being "nebby" means being a nosy busybody—a result of the dark side of bonding social capital (Putnam 2000). But participants also felt that nebbiness, at times, could be important, especially when motivated by a genuine concern for others. "A little bit of nebby might help prevent some of the opioid stuff," said one member of Group A. "So, if you're into the family thing, and there's a family disconnect or dysfunction, it's probably good to know about it." Another participant, who was in recovery, believed that this type of nebbiness is not an intrusion but an essential form of support and encouragement,

> especially when dealing with people with alcohol and substance abuse problems. But I'm very encouraged with the people who live with me, as I live at a three-quarter house, and everyone in the house at this point is doing really well. And it's encouraging, you know? It's hopeful, you know? I, being in recovery myself, take an actual part in helping young men get back on track in life and life's values and life's terms because if you don't know about people with substance abuse problems it can be really bad. Their lives can be completely flipped around as you know through hearing about the opioid addiction problem. . . .
>
> So, for me that has to be at the top of the [list], and then I like nebby, neighborly people. I want to live next to a nebby neighbor who is good to go because believe me they're looking. If somebody comes by your house that doesn't belong, then you're going to know about it.

What keeps nebbiness helpful, they continued, was a commitment to making the community *livable*. "It's always nice to have pride and hope in your community," they said, "but if it's not liveable you can't have any of that." Neighborliness and vigilance, then, were vital, but only when everyone in the community understood that nebby neighbors were interested in the welfare of others and the livability of the community itself—and when those nebby neighbors not only could see when they were overstepping their bounds but also knew how to help, whether that was checking in on elderly neighbors or offering help when local businesses needed it.

In this exchange, Group A was differentiating between what Ronald C. Arnett, Janie M. Harden Fritz, and Leanne M. Bell McManus (2018), following Charles Taylor (1992), call *superordinate* and *subordinate* goods. Although neighborliness and vigilance were important parts of community life, they were not ends unto themselves. They needed to be seen as subordinate to the social goods that the members of Group A felt were more important: livability, active participation, invitation, and community pride and hope (see Table 5.2a).

After the groups narrowed their lists, they worked together to develop a working definition for each social good and envision what Southton would look like if everyone embraced that good in their daily lives. As the following tables suggest, the groups engaged in the tasks slightly differently, with Group A electing to create a single statement and Group B (see Table 5.2b) opting for a more detailed response. Even though the lists were different in structure, they overlapped in interesting ways. For instance, Group A's first social good, *livability*, focused on the importance of creating a supportive community and a beautiful lived environment much like Group B. Moreover, both groups also focused on high levels of participation in community activities. Finally, although Group A was more secularly grounded and Group B more consciously religious, both groups emphasized the importance not only of pride and hope but also of a spirit of invitation that promotes a sense of trust, mutual well-being, and safety.

Group B's more expanded approach to the list is helpful in understanding what this sense of trust, well-being, and safety looks and feels

Table 5.2a Social goods, definitions, and visions for Group A

Social Good	Definition: What does this good mean in your own words?	Vision: What would life in Southton be like if everyone lived this good out in their daily lives?
Livability	Living in a friendly, accessible, caring community with valued and valuable assets.	The community would continue to thrive and grow.
Active Participation	Being actively involved, spending time and improving the community.	Well-attended community meetings, clean streets. Better engagement.
Invitation	Collection of destinations and assets (and people) that make people want to come here and feel welcome.	Safe.
Pride and Hope	Investment in the community with positive expectations and a desire to share the results.	Build trust, friendships. Southton as "standard bearer."

Table 5.2b Social goods, definitions, and visions for Group B

Social Good	Definition: What does this good mean in your own words?	Vision: What would life in Southton be like if everyone lived this good out in their daily lives?
Support	People helping people, taking action when needed, talking with people. Lending a hand, offering to help, being able to ask for help. Looking for ways to serve those in close proximity to you, feeling confident that you can get what you need from others. Helping out when needed, being there for others.	People would have greater bandwidth to meet the challenges in their own lives, greater peace of mind, and generosity would feel more natural. We'd feel safer, friendlier. It would feel that life was more manageable. We could know what one another needs, wants, and cares about.
Community Activities	Shared enjoyments, participating, cooperating with community members. Building blocks of shared culture, living a more integrated life. Doing things together, living a common life, working together, celebrating together, bonding together to do the hard thing. Meetings, conversations, work, fun, friends.	People wouldn't feel as isolated, have a sense of accomplishment, and get to know more people, too. People would feel empowered to bloom where they're planted, and no one would complain that they're bored. It would be fun! More people would be connected, more people in the know about what's going on, and the place would look nicer.
Faith	Drawing on (ideally common) sources outside oneself for fulfillment and decision-making. Belief in God. Believing in what one ought to do and knowing why. Basis of living. Golden rule, sharing values.	It would be a kinder, more caring place. One that took care of its own problems. A safer place. An enjoyable place. And the kind of place you'd let your kids walk around by themselves. More cooperation and kindness. Integrity and joy would be the expectation and the norm.
Environment	Cleaning the community, recognizing problems and solving them. Maintaining property values, safety. Infrastructure that makes community livable and best facilitates our other values. Walkable. Beautiful place, sights, sounds, smells that lighten the spirit and mind; place creating spontaneous community.	More shade trees, more flowers, more time on the front porch. Beautiful, walkable, convenient, facilitates a fun, independent, "relatively" safe and wholesome childhood. Clean but not sterile. Classier, less stressful to see clean streets.

like. Feeling supported, the group contended, would give people more "bandwidth" to deal with the stressfulness of their lives, helping them feel safer and readier to connect with one another through community activities, especially activities that affirm deeper values. These connections, they hoped, would make Southton a place where people could "bloom where they're planted," a comment that seems to reflect the lingering pain of the death of the steel industry in the 1980s and the flight of young people from the region (Hoerr 1988). Finally, echoing Eric Klinenberg's (2018) discussion of social infrastructure, they emphasized the importance of the local environment, especially trees, litter-free sidewalks, and green spaces that not only make the streets more beautiful but also reduce the stress that people experience on a daily basis.

At the end of the session, participants were asked to set aside about 30 minutes over the following week to think about these social goods and complete a short questionnaire. For each good, they were asked to answer three questions: *How is this good already being lived out around me? What obstacles might get in the way of living out these goods? What can I, or we, do—right now—as individuals or as a community to live out these goods in our everyday lives?* As before, this exercise was optional and offered with the expectation that some participants would feel more comfortable writing than others. How or whether participants completed the task was less important than giving them the opportunity to think about the social goods they believed held Southton together.

Session Three: Engaging Apathy and Adult Bullying

The third session emphasized designing practices that participants thought could help them live out the social goods they had defined during the previous two weeks. To start the conversation, the participants engaged in a traditional "Rose-Bud-Thorn" exercise that helped them focus on Southton's established strengths that could help residents live out its social goods (Roses), potential strengths that could be developed to help live out those goods (Buds), and the obstacles that get in the way of those goods (Thorns). The results of this exercise (see Table 5.3a) point to a complex picture. Although the two groups' respective lists differed considerably, both saw strength in Southton as an active, friendly community. Moreover, they saw potential strengths in the neighborhood's physical infrastructure—vacant storefronts to be renovated, traffic patterns to be improved, green spaces to be beautified, and community gardens to be planted.

Table 5.3a Results of the "Rose-Bud-Thorn" exercise (frequency of responses in parentheses)

	Group A	Group B
Roses	Active participation in community events (4)	People out on sidewalks and Main Street (3)
	Little League and soccer coaching (2)	Friendly businesses and neighbors (3)
	Southton Teen Outreach (2)	Police cooperation/public safety (2)
	Outgoing people (2)	Active churches (2)
		Common landmarks and green spaces (2)
		Community values education/families (2)
	Others: Southton's wall; clean streets; good attendance at Southton Together meetings	*Others:* Well-attended events; art and theater programs; residents pick up litter; affordable housing; variety of ages; variety of activities
Buds	Cleaner storefronts and streets (2)	Parks/community garden/green spaces (5)
	Public transportation/traffic patterns (2)	Vacant storefronts/underused facilities (4)
		Opportunities for caring volunteers (3)
		Sports equipment and leagues (2)
	Others: Disconnected from key resources; police substations; activities for kids; empty storefronts following up on negative news events	Block parties and local events (2)
		Others: Transportation; block watch; Southton newsletter; childcare databases
Thorns	Money and taxes (2)	Adult bullies/cliques/infighting (5)
	Lack of involvement (2)	Litter/uneven sidewalks (3)
	Landlords/others not keeping up property (2)	Apathy/unwillingness to change (3)
	Too few non-bars (2)	Business vacancies/blighted properties (2)
		Not enough non-bars open after 5:00 p.m. (2)
	Others: Traffic; crime; current resources/people overcommitted	*Others:* Bad/unfocused planning; no shade trees; people distracted by cell phones; fewer buses after 10:00 p.m.; lack of access to information; lack of outreach to marginalized people; traffic goes too fast; culture of staying inside; culture of going outside the neighborhood; opioids

Yet, groups also noticed significant problems simmering under the surface. Southton's businesses were not always family-friendly, and many of these businesses did not seem to be doing their part to keep the neighborhood clean and livable. Even more important, the groups pointed to a pervading sense of apathy within the community that translated into a lack of involvement in community groups and initiatives. Group B was particularly focused on this point, describing this culture as one defined by adult bullying, cliques, and infighting that belied the friendly image projected at community events.

Based on these insights, the groups brainstormed practices designed to help them strengthen a current strength, build up a potential strength, or overcome obstacles. Working in partners, the participants began with a social good and then, with that good in mind, picked a Rose, Bud, or Thorn from their respective lists. Building on Kemmis, McTaggart, and Nixon's (2014) definition of a practice, the partners suggested a specific, concrete way of saying, doing, or relating that could enhance the Rose, develop the Bud, or address the Thorn. After designing the practices, the partners proposed each to the group. If the group thought it made sense, they kept it. The point of the exercise was not to develop a polished list but to generate five to seven practices that would be the basis for their "homework" during the following week.

The tentative list of practices for Group A (see Table 5.3b) and Group B (see Table 5.3c) closely supported social goods. Between the two groups, clear patterns emerged around picking up litter, engaging strangers in friendly ways, and supporting local businesses.

Table 5.3b Tentative list of practices for Group A

Good	Practice	Attending to What Matters	Being Present	Caring for the Common
Livability	• Pick up a piece of litter every day.	✓		✓
	• Engage with five people every day that you've never met before.	✓	✓	
Active Participation	• Support youth athletic leagues by volunteering, fundraising, and spectating.		✓	✓
Invitation	• Shop more at our local businesses and talk about it!		✓	✓
Pride and Hope	• Talk with a neighbor every day.	✓	✓	

Table 5.3c Tentative list of practices for Group B

Good	Practice	Attending to What Matters	Being Present	Caring for the Common
Support	• Do one random act of kindness every day.		✓	✓
	• Talk to someone new as you go about your routines.	✓	✓	
Community Activities	• Seek out and put on the calendar upcoming community events and remind others of those events in everyday conversation.	✓		✓
Faith	• Notice adult bullies and call them out.	✓		✓
	• Comfort grieving families.		✓	
	• Read the obituaries.	✓	✓	
Environment	• Support local businesses.		✓	✓
	• Pick up one piece of litter a day.	✓		✓

Interestingly, virtually all of the practices spoke to multiple facets of communal literacy. For instance, picking up litter, which both groups mentioned, is a form of attending to the social good of livability as well as an act that cares for the common spaces where people live their lives, while engaging with strangers requires people both to pay attention to the social good of supportiveness and to be present to others by exchanging a kind word. This is an important insight since it suggests the possibility of "super practices" that address multiple components of communal literacy simultaneously.

One of the most interesting exchanges came in Group B when it came to an initiative to respond to bullying, an issue that three group members felt particularly passionate about:

[B1]: We're going to start campaigning against adult bullying. We want to start that.

[FACILITATOR]: So what is a way you could do that?

[B1]: The easiest way is to set up meetings with adults who have been bullied and see if we can solve their problems. And ask around and see if there are people who would want to join us.

[FACILITATOR]: So if we were to break that down even smaller, is there a way we could do that?

[B6]: We were talking about calling it out.

[B2]: Stick up for people.

[B1]: If you see someone being a bully, say hey, you know. Don't be afraid to support the person who is being bullied. Adult bullies. We can all find kids who are bullies, but those kids grow up, some of them grow up to be exactly what they were when they were young.

[B3]: Sometimes bullies, they bully employees. Like in the restaurant, like waitresses, the staff. I consider that bullying.

[B2]: My next-door neighbor had a work crew, in the digger thing, he just yelled and screamed and berated the other workmen all day long. So I went and talked to the owner of the property.

Such a strong focus on adult bullying is striking, but it makes sense given the climate of trauma, stigmatization, and verbal aggression discussed earlier. As Faye Mishna and Melissa van Wert (2014) observe, bullying is an omnipresent fact of contemporary life both in person and online, but the current conversation on bullying typically sees the problem as something experienced and perpetrated by young people, not adults. Yet, as Renee L. Cowan (2013) observes—and the members of Group B attested—adults engage just as often as young people in verbal and nonverbal behaviors that reasonable observers would find inappropriate, toxic, or abusive. The difference, she writes, is that adult bullying in the workplace and elsewhere is often hidden behind explanations and excuses: that some people simply have a more aggressive communication style than others, that their communication skills are just flawed, that the culture or social environment makes it inevitable, or that bullying behavior is nothing more than a personality clash. Although these rationalizations for adult bullying may make sense to the people making these excuses—whether they are observers, victims, or perpetrators—they also allow for the toxic practice to remain invisible.

The invisibility of adult bullying makes Group B's emphasis on *noticing* important. Noticing calls upon the capacity to attend to what matters, a central facet of communal literacy. But noticing is only the first step. Bystanders also need to be present to victims of bullying and, in turn, care for the common spaces where this toxic behavior is occurring. "Bystanders," writes Laura Martocci (2015, 145), are uniquely positioned "to sort significant social slights and devastating public rejections from the routine ups and downs of everyday life" because they can contextualize the exchange, understand what is wrong, and address it. Yet, assuming that role brings risks, Martocci argues, and not simply because the bully can easily turn their energies on the intervening bystander. Simply witnessing bullying behavior can be just as harmful to the bystander as it is to the victim, she notes, and this discomfort is what encourages people to make bullying invisible through the very explanations and excuses that Cowan (2013) describes. Indeed, because bystanders are as embedded in the situation as bullies and their victims are, we can also see them as experiencing the same pressures and traumas that victims are feeling. As a result, Martocci contends, bystanders often need just as much support as the victims they are trying to help.

This point underscores how complex and challenging an apparently simple micropractice can be—and how much support people might need to practice them well. The member of Group B who intervened with the property owner because they were concerned about how the head of a work crew was treating the rest of the team was practicing the social good of "faith" as they understood it by speaking up for the dignity of the members of the work crew. Yet, in the transcript, the participant's story unfortunately stopped there. They gave no information about how the foreman and the work team responded or whether they were successful in changing the underlying dynamics of the situation. Perhaps the discomfort of the subject prompted the other members of Group B to move on. The ambiguity, though, says volumes about the vulnerability found in the practice of community life today. When practicing community, people have no idea whether their efforts will be successful, reciprocated, or even accepted. Practicing community, as suggested earlier, is humble work that can only wait for the roots of community to grow (Maier 2013). This insight certainly underscores the daily discipline of life together, but it also calls attention to the extensive support those who are practicing community need to have. In this sense, the institutions and the everyday practices that sustain a community seem to rise and fall together, a relationship that became even more apparent during the next session.

As the session drew to a close, participants were invited to put the practices they designed to the test over the following week. Like the week before, each participant received a sheet upon which they were to note why they chose the practice, what happened when they tested it, and what they learned from the experience. This learning would drive the following session, in which the vulnerability of micropractices took center stage.

Session Four: Seeking a "Culture of Kindness"

After the previous week's work, the fourth session sought to achieve two goals. First, the inquiry groups worked together to unpack their experiences testing the practices they designed during the previous session and use that information to refine their list of practices. Then, after a short break, the groups engaged in an exercise called "Upstairs/Downstairs," in which they examined interactions between people with differing levels of authority. This section will describe each exercise in turn.

Refining Practices

As participants recounted their experiences, some found that living out their practices was more challenging than they expected. For instance, the members of Group B, who focused in part on adult bullying, found that calling out adult bullies can be daunting, especially because those engaging in bullying behavior may become defensive and act aggressively in response. But even more important, they reported feeling that even if they did succeed in putting a social good into practice, their efforts would be ultimately futile. As one exchange suggested, littering seemed like an especially lost cause in a neighborhood that seemed steeped in disrespect and hostility:

[B1]: It was interesting trying to do every [practice we designed], every day because I decided to do them all. It was very interesting trying to do everything every day. It was really interesting. As far as picking up the litter was concerned, I did it every day, I didn't make a dent anywhere, in anything. Yes, I know, it means it wasn't any worse than it was before, but I just feel there seems to be an educational, a lack of an educational component that needs to go into that. Why do people throw anything away?

[B3]: A lack of respect. Being aware, or hostility, sometimes. Even though the waste can's right here, I'm going to do it, let somebody else do it.

[B1]: I know, it's crazy.

Group B struggled on this point throughout their discussion. In fact, the group members seem to have decided to remove the micropractice focusing on picking up litter from their final list (see Table 5.4b), suggesting that they believed that Southton's problem with litter, while important, was too much of a challenge for a single person to tackle.

One member of Group B in particular felt that the practices themselves were too scattered. They pushed back on the practice of engaging in "random acts of kindness" each day, not because they were against being kind to others but because they felt the practice was so unfocused that it was unworkable. "I guess what I'm disputing is this notion of the 'random' act," they said. "Shouldn't it be expected that people treat each other kindly or that kind things occur between strangers?" The discussion proceeded from there, with the other group members emphasizing the importance of being kind in a world where people can live their lives without encountering any kindness whatsoever. These acts, the other group members argued, bend back on the giver as well, changing both the giver and the receiver. When the critical member asked them to give an example of their experiences, one participant talked about encountering a young boy who was carrying home a school art project they found particularly beautiful and another incident when they met a woman begging for money on the street:

[B1]: I gave him the money to buy a portfolio. God knows if he bought one or not, but it made me feel better. One night there was a woman who was begging for money on the street and she said she was hungry and her kids were hungry and I said, "Fine, let's go to McDonald's." So I went to McDonald's and said, "You can order anything you want," and I bought it for her, and then I walked away and left. Not knowing whether she was going to eat it, or sell it. But the fact that I was kind to her, I hope had an influence on her.

[B3]: Sometimes it's the smallest little thing. Like when you go down to Aldi's someone will give you a quarter for your cart so you don't have to put that quarter in, and you feel good, and they feel good, and you say "pass it on." And they smile, especially if that person has a baby, they're putting the baby in the chair in the car and they have the groceries and they don't want to leave the baby there and take the cart back, and that sort of . . . that little thing makes their life easier and everyone feels better. And it's so small! Such a small thing.

[B2]: That really matters. That really makes a difference.

[B6]: If everyone did that, and no one cared about the quarter, then . . .

[B1]: Then we wouldn't need random acts of kindness.

In an interesting way, the members of Group B were describing how virtuous micropractices—a supportive smile here, a quarter or two there, a small gift given without any strings attached—translate into a broader social vision. What is essential here is that the group members understood the *object* of these practices—the smile, the quarter, the gift—to be less important to both the giver and the receiver than the *purpose* of the practice itself.

But if no one cares about the random act of kindness, what do they care about? The discussion continued:

[B2]: Does it need to be more specific or more challenging or? Or we don't actually value kindness, what specifically is the problem?

[B6]: I think it sets the bar too low, almost. To do these things that are above and beyond presupposes that we are not doing kind things to one another to begin with. That, that's kind of what I'm getting at, it kind of sets the normal bar too low, as long as you have one random act of kindness, you can act like a jerk the rest of the time. I don't know that that's exactly right, I think there should be a culture of kindness, or something along those lines.

Creating a "culture of kindness" seemed key here in situating the micropractices they were designing in a broader story that all the participants seemed to be trying to tell. In the context of Group B's discussion, the outline of this story is simple: *We live in a place where people aren't kind to one another. We want to create a culture of kindness. How can we help each other be more kind?* This story was powerful because it not only pointed to a future that the group members found compelling, but it also suggested an improvisational "stage" in which people could interact with each other.

We can see the finalized list of practices for Group A (Table 5.4a) and Group B (Table 5.4b) as giving an outline of what this stage might look like. In many respects, the finalized list looks much like the list from before, with some minor tweaks in language. The consistency suggests that, after a week of experimentation, participants believed that most of the practices they designed were doable and potentially helpful. Together, too, they show how closely a community of kindness is tied to the practice of communal literacy. A kind community, in other words, is one where members know how to pay attention to people and goods around them, support their lives together, and care for what they share together, whether that is through participating in youth athletic leagues, patronizing local businesses, comforting the families of people who have died, picking up litter, or acknowledging strangers on the street.

Table 5.4a Final list of practices for Group A

Good	Practice	Attending to What Matters	Being Present	Caring for the Common
Livability	• Pick up a piece of litter every day.	✓		✓
	• Say "Hi" and acknowledge people in the community.	✓	✓	✓
Active Participation	• Support youth athletic leagues by volunteering, fundraising, and spectating.		✓	✓
Invitation	• Know, talk about, and advocate for our local businesses and assets.	✓	✓	✓
Pride and Hope	• Talk with "neighbors" during the week.	✓	✓	

Yet, participants noted that living out these practices can be challenging, especially when not everyone agrees on what being kind is, is aware of how kindness is practiced within a community, or is in a position to pay attention, support, or care for others. One participant described a situation where they offered their seat to a woman on the bus, who promptly yelled at them to mind their own business. Experiences like this can make people think twice about offering kindness in a time of difference. The experience, the participant continued, reminds us that being kind can be both awkward and nerve-wracking because it means taking the risk of making a mistake. "So these random acts of kindness require a certain, again as I said, willingness to be awkward, right?" they said. "I would consider that a certain humility in the sense that you might just humiliate yourself by helping someone in a certain way that he could be totally rejected flat on his face." In seeking to create and foster a culture of kindness, the giver's overtures can be rejected, leaving them hurt, while the receiver must be willing to be vulnerable enough to accept the kindness in the first place.

Table 5.4b Final list of practices for Group **B**

Good	Practice	Attending to What Matters	Being Present	Caring for the Common
Support	• Do at least one random act of kindness every day in order to develop a culture of kindness.	✓	✓	✓
	• Talk to someone new as you go about your routines.	✓	✓	✓
Community Activities	• Seek out and put on the calendar upcoming community events and remind others of those events in everyday conversation.	✓		✓
Faith	• Notice adult bullies and call them out.	✓		
	• Comfort grieving families, read the obituaries, and pray for the dead.	✓	✓	✓
Environment	• Support local businesses by getting in the habit of asking, "Can I buy this in Southton?"		✓	✓

Upstairs/Downstairs

The delicate balance of power between givers and receivers speaks to the issue that the "Upstairs/Downstairs" exercise strived to address. Until then, the discussion had focused on everyday exchanges between people who are more or less on the same level. But many important conversations occur between people who are at different places in the hierarchy that could be called "upstairs/downstairs" encounters: managers and subordinates, state funding agencies and nonprofits, nonprofits and community members, police officers and citizens, nurses and patients, parents and children, or teachers and students. The research team chose to add this particular exercise to the study because of the tensions that many neighborhoods had experienced between residents and the government agencies and nonprofits tasked with responding to the opioid epidemic, some of which were discussed in previous chapters.

During this exercise, participants were asked to think about a situation from their own experience living or working in Southton in which they saw two people at differing levels communicating well with each other to solve a mutual problem or a conflict between them. The situation could have been an interaction they saw happen or something they experienced directly. The participants were asked to write or tell the story in the third person (i.e., not "I said to her . . ." or "She said to me . . ." but "The social worker said to the client . . .") to provide a degree of distance between themselves and the story they were telling. After describing the issue and what the people did to respond to it, participants were asked to imagine, as best they could, what each person thought or felt and describe what made the interaction successful.

Both groups provided a variety of stories, which they then read aloud to the rest of the group. The members of Group A, for example, discussed a shop owner intervening with a rowdy customer, a coach addressing a player on a losing soccer team, and a passerby talking with a young person riding a bike in a reckless and destructive way. These situations could easily have escalated or left one or both of the actors feeling hurt, but they did not. In fact, they ended in ways that seemed to leave both actors feeling valued by the other. What made the difference?

For the members of Group A, the key seemed to be the person in the "upstairs" position. As the person with the greater level of authority, their responsibility was to *model* the type of encounter they wanted to have, to "be" the kindness and respect they wanted to give and receive from the other person. In practice, modeling meant learning to find ways to control anger and frustration enough to listen and allow for a conversation where both people could engage each other as equals. In other words, instead of telling the other what to do, the "upstairs" person had the responsibility to come "downstairs" to see the situation from the opposing point of view. Making that imaginative journey, even for a moment, allowed for both parties to leave the conversation better. As the members of Group A said:

[A7]: The downstairs person walked away having had a positive experience. So they weren't mad or sad or angry. And probably without making a decision they were performing the way upstairs people wanted them to perform.

[FACILITATOR]: So what made the anger or the shame not there?

[A1]: It was a conversation rather than one person telling the other person. It wasn't a demand; it was a conversation that happened. And so it wasn't just the upstairs person being heard. The downstairs [person] was heard as well. Or felt heard.

Based on these discussions, participants described the attributes of successful "upstairs" and "downstairs" actors. Although their lists differed considerably, members of both Group A and Group B believed that successful "upstairs" actors modeled empathy, listening, and respect through a tone that met the "downstairs" actors where they were and did not belittle them or resort to shouting or other forms of verbal and physical violence. Successful "downstairs" actors, on the other hand, returned this respect by journeying "up" the ladder, engaging with what the "upstairs" actors had to say and empathizing with it, even if it meant correcting their own behavior. With the "upstairs" actors coming "down" and the downstairs actors coming "up," the two could act as equals, acknowledging each other's vulnerability, assuming the best in each other, sharing their thoughts, feelings, and expectations, and leaving the interaction feeling heard.

This vision of mutual kindness and respect between "upstairs" and "downstairs" actors mirrored the culture of kindness the participants wanted to create for themselves. This insight drove the final inquiry assignment, which asked participants to consider what Southton would look like if everyone lived these practices—and the social goods they supported—to the fullest. As before, they received a worksheet that could collect their thoughts.

Session Five: The "Mystery of Southton"

The final session completed the discussion by returning to the questions that some of the participants in the 2017 study (Maier 2018) found difficult to answer: What might Southton look like if everyone practiced community together? And what actions might it take for the community to make that vision a reality? Instead of asking these questions outright, however, the inquiry groups employed a methodology called *community mapping*, an approach developed by social psychologists Valerie A. Futch and Michelle Fine (2013). Then, the participants engaged in an action planning exercise, where they brainstormed potential actions that the community as a whole could take to support its life together.

Community Mapping

In community mapping, participants receive a sheet of paper and art supplies and are asked to create a drawing that depicts an aspect of their everyday lives or a dimension of their community they want to share with others. Although the quality of the drawings varies depending on the artistic abilities of the participants, the point of the exercise is not to create works of art. Allowing people to express complex thoughts and ideas, these drawings, or "community maps," are instead intended to open conversation and prompt new ways of thinking (Futch and Fine 2013). Within the context of the session, participants were given 15 minutes to draw their own individual visions of what Southton would look like if everyone lived the social goods and practices that they had been discussing over the previous four weeks. When they were finished, each inquiry group worked together to merge their individual drawings into a single image. Group A's image (see Figure 5.1a) emerged from an energetic discussion and depicted what members saw as a vibrant, connected neighborhood, in which everyone could engage and know one another. Central to this vision was a revitalized, walkable main street with green trees surrounded by family-centric, supportive institutions like swimming pools, houses, ball fields, and a grocery store—symbols of vibrancy and self-sufficiency.

Group B also focused on a revitalized Southton Boulevard (see Figure 5.1b), showing that, for both groups, this main street remained the defining symbol of the neighborhood. The drawing shows a different mix of buildings, including vibrant businesses, stores where people could buy anything they needed locally, creatively used spaces, gardens, community centers, and churches. The sidewalks are important, as well. They are broad, full of places to sit and meet as well as green trees, and they line a street that is safe enough for families to walk safely. In this regard, Group B, like Group A, emphasized many of the core points that Eric Klinenberg (2018) makes about social infrastructure. It was clear that their vision of a revitalized Southton required significant investments in physical places where strangers could meet and develop relationships with each other. Streets need to be clean and green—indeed, the color green was a prominent visual theme in both drawings—sidewalks need to be wide and inviting, local businesses and community organizations need to be strong, and parks, ball fields, and swimming pools need to be open for people to gather. All of these assets give shape to social connections.

But the discussion in both groups went beyond the physical assets to describe the practices occurring and social goods being sustained within that space. One of the members of Group A noted that the common theme in their group's discussion was connection and engagement. The opioid epidemic brought the lack of these things to light. "So you're engaged," they said, "you're probably not sitting in the corner having the blues, right?" They continued:

> If you're connected, that's gonna do a lot to fix that piece, which is what started this process. And I've told this story before, I'll

Figure 5.1a Final drawing from Group A

tell it again: My next door neighbor's son, okay, turned 18 or 20 or something like that, and he got his own apartment down the block. Big celebration, right? His dad's a painter, so his dad went and painted his apartment. Big deal! Very exciting thing, right? He got himself a roommate. Two months later, he was dead with an overdose. He was not a user. So, his connection changed, and

Figure 5.1b Final drawing from Group B

he didn't open a new connection. Very sad thing, twenty years old.
Only two months out of his own bedroom at home. Bad scene.

The other part of the engagement, so that's engagement within the
community, but the other part of the engagement that jumps out to
me, is I wear a t-shirt often that has Southton on it with a zip code
and a couple of other things. I always, no matter what part of the city
I'm in, get questions about it, "Hey, I'm from Southton, or I know
somebody in Southton! Did you know that da da da da da . . .?"

So, the whole mystery of Southton, the reaction that I get most
often, when I say I'm from Southton is, "I didn't know that Southton has, does, is, whatever." I didn't know. That's the whole thing.
That's the engagement piece. I couldn't resist. The big picture is
solving the "I didn't know" piece about Southton. External to the
neighborhood.

This story emphasizes the importance of human connection *within* the
social infrastructure for building relationships both within and outside
of the community. The social infrastructure may facilitate connection
and engagement, but it cannot replace the invisible value connection
and engagement bring to people's lives. In a sense, that sense of value
is what the participant captured in the phrase, "the whole mystery of
Southton": There is something in the neighborhood that is powerful,

even though it might not be readily apparent by looking at the current state of its streets.

For locals, the presence or absence of connection—as we see in the story of the young man who moved out of the supportive environment of his family and died two months later from an overdose—can hold decisive importance for their lives. For those outside of the neighborhood, who may look at Southton Boulevard and see only a line of bars, payday lenders, and litter, not paying attention to these invisible bonds can lead them to dismiss the neighborhood's potential, an attitude that can prompt adverse types of "upstairs/downstairs" encounters that generate only hostility and resistance. The members of both groups could clearly see this mystery and what deepening it could bring for the community. Group B's picture in particular seems to be trying to spell it out, not only by depicting the people who are on the streets but also by providing detailed labels describing the types of engagements they aspired to see: intergenerational relationships of mentoring and support, people interested in and eager to promote community events, shopping patterns that support local businesses, adults willing and trusted enough to look after other people's children, children who are growing up to be self-sufficient, relaxed and supportive families who enjoy each other's company, and visible firefighters and police officers who are eating ice cream because the neighborhood is so safe their services are never needed.

In a sense, both groups' drawings depicted a complex, reciprocal relationship between the visible, physical presence of social infrastructure and the invisible "mysteries" of social connectedness that bring that infrastructure to life. Obviously, there seemed to be a deep awareness of the importance of social infrastructure as Klinenberg (2018) would describe it. But without a strong web of social connection, these community assets can easily fall into disrepair. And it was clear that even as they desired the external investment and support necessary to build the social infrastructure they needed, participants also believed that internal action was necessary to recreate social connectedness. This distinction can help understand the action planning that followed. Social infrastructure is an intervention that comes from the outside. Social connectedness and social capital are mysteries that emerge from within.

Action Planning

In keeping with the principles of PCI, the action planning focused on things the participants themselves wanted to commit to doing or thought that the community could do on its own, instead of looking for help from outside institutions. To assist with the action planning, participants walked through the W. K. Kellogg Foundation's (2004) logic model framework. After brainstorming potential actions that they believed would help move Southton toward the future they wanted to see, they selected one and considered the outputs the action would create, the desired outcomes emerging from that action, the impact that they hoped to achieve, and the resources that they believed would be necessary for the action to succeed.

Although both groups brainstormed several actions, the limited time remaining in the session meant that they could begin to develop a model for only one. Both groups focused on communication actions designed to support the social goods and practices that they had been discussing. Interestingly, both Group A (see Table 5.5a) and Group B (see Table 5.5b) focused on the importance of having a centralized hub of information, albeit in different ways. Group A emphasized the development of a web and social media presence to provide information so that people could know what was going on in the community, while Group B desired to create community-based communication initiatives designed to help people learn how to engage each other. Group B in particular believed that residents needed assistance with not only connecting to events and resources but also navigating the complex social and interpersonal environment around them. How do you create a block party? What do you need to create a community garden? How do you talk to an unaccompanied teenager who is out too late at night—without calling the police or children and youth services? What does it mean to be a good neighbor?

During the discussion, the members of Group B noted that while the Pittsburgh city government and numerous other nonprofit organizations have their own series of handouts, these resources need to be home-grown. "I just want to stress, I think it's very important that these things feel local, not imposed, like they were organically created by people who want them and know about them," one said. "Because they're your neighbors rather than from someone pushing an agenda from outside." Although the inquiry groups concluded after this meeting, this insight suggested that the inquiry could have easily gone into the future, with participants working together to bring these action plans to fruition.

The framework of bonding and bridging actions can help interpret this action planning in interesting ways. On the one hand, Group A chose to focus on a bridging action designed to give information to the community as a whole, instead of focusing more on bonding-related

Table 5.5a Group A's logic model

Action	Outputs	Outcomes	Impact	Resources
Create official channels of communication (website, newsletter, etc.)	Webmaster Curated list of events History, pictures Links to organizations, Facebook pages, websites	Business, families, visitors will know about events More volunteers and greater attendance at community events (meetings, fundraisers, festivals)	New stores, restaurants, activities More work can get done Volunteer opportunities New neighbors Higher property value New (Catholic) schools More bars/clubs More taxes for upkeep Crowded schools	Webmaster/group with skills Money Expertise

Other actions considered: Create a welcoming committee; rekindle block watch (more volunteers/neighbors); creating and helping with community events

Table 5.5b Group B's logic model

Action	Outputs	Outcomes	Impact	Resources
Brochure series developed by community members, for community members	Create block party How to make a community garden How to talk to unaccompanied teenagers How to plant trees How to be a good neighbor Directory of resources	Start conversations Getting more people involved Eliminate negative feelings, e.g., toward teenagers Increased use of resources	Litter Advertising local businesses Peace of mind Improved communication	Local researchers and writers Involvement from community groups Information from city Place to display them

Other actions considered: Initiatives to improve walkability; community garden; more outdoor seating

actions like creating a welcoming committee or reinvigorating the local block watch. The group felt that many of these initiatives were already occurring but needed to be drawn together and coordinated at
a community level. "One of the things that I've put in my little list is
that there is a lot of stuff going on, like the diminishing block watch,
for example," one member said. "But how many people realize that
it's diminishing? So, there needs to be a communication thing, and I
don't know what form that takes." Newsletters developed by various
community groups existed, they continued, but there was no central,
trusted place where organizations and residents could share information that was important to them. Here, the group felt the level of
bonding social capital was high. What was necessary was finding ways
to bridge between groups within the community to help them move
forward.

The action Group B proposed, however, was a bit more complex,
because the brochure series had aspects that were both bonding and
bridging in nature. On one hand, the group members felt Southton
needed resources oriented toward bonding: Creating a community garden, throwing a block party, or being a good neighbor, for instance, all
seem to be focused on strengthening ties between people who already
have relationships with each other. At the same time, however, other
resources, particularly the resource on how to have conversations with
unaccompanied teenagers instead of calling the cops, seem designed
to reach across boundaries—obviously age but potentially also race
and class—in ways that build bridges between people. Each of these
resources, individually focused on a different task and purpose, seems
to be an action in its own right. While Group A emphasized a single,
large project, Group B was heading toward a smaller, more iterative
approach that targeted specific community communication needs.
Thinking big or thinking small, both groups together suggested concrete interventions promoting social connectedness, illustrating the
potential of PCI to help a community in crisis to heal.

References

Arnett, Ronald C., Janie M. Harden Fritz, and Leeanne M. Bell McManus.
2018. *Communication Ethics Literacy: Dialogue and Difference.* 2nd ed.
Dubuque, IA: Kendall Hunt Publishing.

Cowan, Renee L. 2013. "'**it Rolls Downhill' and Other Attributions for Why
Adult Bullying Happens in Organizations from the Human Resource Professional's Perspective." *Qualitative Research Reports in Communication* 14,
no. 1: 97–104. https://doi.org/10.1080/17459435.2013.835347.

Futch, Valerie A., and Michelle Fine. 2013. "Mapping as a Method: History and Theoretical Commitments." *Qualitative Research in Psychology* 11, no. 1: 42–59. https://doi.org/10.1080/14780887.2012.719070.

Hoerr, John. 1988. *And the Wolf Finally Came: The Decline and Fall of the American Steel Industry.* Pittsburgh, PA: University of Pittsburgh Press.

Kemmis, Stephen, Robin McTaggart, and Rhonda Nixon. 2014. *The Action Research Planner: Doing Critical Participatory Action Research.* New York: Springer.

Klinenberg, Eric. 2018. *Palaces for the People: How Social Infrastructure Can Help Fight Inequality, Polarization, and the Decline of Civic Life.* New York: Crown.

MacIntyre, Alasdair. 2007. *After Virtue: A Study in Moral Theory.* 3rd ed. South Bend, IN: University of Notre Dame Press.

Maier, Craig T. 2013. "Attentive Waiting in an Uprooted Age: Simone Weil's Response in an Age of Precarity." *Review of Communication* 13, no. 3: 225–42. https://doi.org/10.1080/15358593.2013.843715.

———. 2018. "Light and Shadows: Appreciative Inquiry, Communication Ethics Literacy, and the Opioid Epidemic." *Qualitative Research Reports in Communication* 19, no. 1: 62–67. https://doi.org/10.1080/17459435.2018.1529699.

Maier, Craig T., and David DeIuliis. 2015. "Putting the 'Human' in the Human Network: Engaging Digital Business Discourse Through Communicology." In *Digital Business Discourse*, edited by Erica Darics, 208–25. New York: Palgrave Macmillan.

Martocci, Laura. 2015. *Bullying: The Social Destruction of Self.* Philadelphia, PA: Temple University Press.

Mishna, Faye, and Melissa van Wert. 2014. "Bullying." In *Handbook of Social Work Practice with Vulnerable and Resilient Populations*, edited by Alex Gitterman, 227–47. New York: Columbia University Press.

Putnam, Robert. 2000. *Bowling Alone: The Collapse and Revival of American Community.* New York: Simon & Schuster.

Taylor, Charles. 1992. *Sources of the Self.* Cambridge, MA: Harvard University Press.

W. K. Kellogg Foundation. 2004. *Logic Model Development Guide.* Battle Creek, MI: W. K. Kellogg Foundation.

6 Discussion, Limitations, and Recommendations for Practice

This research project sought to frame and test a collaborative research framework called Participatory Community Inquiry (PCI) within the context of the opioid epidemic. Working with two inquiry groups over the course of five weeks, the research team explored how PCI, as an intentionally appreciative, practice-driven, action-oriented approach to community engagement, might lead to transformation in a community that had been especially affected not only by opioid use disorder but also the lingering effects of Rust Belt economic decline and community-level trauma. While the duration of the study was too short and the scope too limited to lead to any definitive policy outcomes, the depth and energy of discussion suggest that PCI may be a promising approach for communities in crisis. This chapter explores the potential for PCI that the study exposed, limitations that need to be addressed in future studies, and recommendations for practice both in Southton and in future applications of the PCI framework.

The Potential for PCI

The flow of the discussion in the two groups, as well as their outputs, suggests that the linkage of appreciative acknowledgment, practice-making and action planning is promising. The quality of the discussion in particular underscored the importance of beginning from an appreciative intent. The difficulties experienced during recruitment, as well as reports from participants throughout the process, suggested that the Southton community was a challenging environment in which people felt uneasy about discussing controversial or painful issues like the opioid epidemic. Focusing attention on what they valued most about the community instead of the pain that they felt opened a space where they could engage each other and work together to think about the problems that they faced in their lives together.

DOI: 10.4324/9781003243663-7

Likewise, the focus on practices seemed important in helping participants learn to respond to an overwhelmingly complex problem. While the members of Group A recognized that they could do little to solve the problem of litter as a whole, they could control the litter they saw on the street. While the members of Group B understood that stopping adult bullying was extraordinarily hard, they could notice it more and try to intervene. And while they could not change the communication climate of the community as a whole, both groups could control how they communicated with others, whether those "others" were strangers on the street, people struggling with substance use disorder, or teenagers making too much noise far too late on a school night.

Together, these practices advanced a vision of the community of kindness, in which people paid attention to each other, were present in each other's lives, and could acknowledge and care for the things that tied them together as neighbors and as people—capacities central to communal literacy. This vision led to clear action steps designed to provide people with the information and the skills they needed to be good citizens and neighbors in a changing neighborhood striving to emerge from crisis. And it was clear that the process was fostering social learning and, had the project continued, would have continued to do so. PCI had encouraged the participants to see their community differently, ask new questions that helped them understand their lives together in new ways, and design practices and actions that can strengthen and invite new stories about their common life. The challenge, however, is how to strengthen, deepen, and sustain this learning so it can foster the changes in Southton that the participants wanted to see.

Limitations

To be sure, the application of PCI within this project is not the only way of implementing the approach. Different facilitation designers and community organizers can employ a variety of means to develop forums that are appreciative in intent, practice-driven, and action-oriented and that draw from a variety of areas of research and practice, including design thinking, story work (Kurtz 2014), large-scale facilitation approaches such as World Café, and community development strategies. But beyond differences in framework, the current study had several limitations that should be addressed in further research and implementations of the approach.

First, the most obvious limitation lies in the size and racial and demographic homogeneity of the inquiry groups. For PCI to work properly, the inquiry groups need to draw from a diversity of races, ethnicities, genders, social classes, and professional roles. The homogeneity in this study was the unintentional result of the recruitment difficulties the team encountered, as well as the racial homogeneity of Southton in general, and the composition of the inquiry groups may have made the discussion easier than it might have been had they been more mixed. What is more, the lack of racial and ethnic diversity within the groups may have unintentionally led to practices and actions that strengthen the exclusionary, darker side of social capital instead of fostering a community in which everyone feels welcome (Putnam 2000). As a result, further exploration of PCI needs to occur within more heterogeneous settings to explore the generative role diversity can play in shaping community-level responses to adversity and deepening the impact of those initiatives.

In addition, future applications of PCI require more time to allow for the discussion to develop more fully. Because of the scope of the study, time presented an important limitation. The protocol included several activities that could have taken much longer, resulting in clearer positions, sharper practices, and better action steps. Lengthening the study, of course, creates its own problems with attrition and recruitment, since many potential participants, especially from marginalized communities, may not be able to attend regularly. Even so, expanding the timeline for the study would allow for the inquiry groups to deepen the cycle of planning, experimenting, and social learning that is so central to action research.

Finally, the current study was limited by a lack of clear strategies to assess both the quality of the outcomes and the depth of participants' social learning. Because of the current study's time constraints, the action phase was truncated, prohibiting the inquiry groups from developing their logic models and testing them in practice. Both groups provided action steps that seemed worth following, and not only because they could impact the Southton community for the better. The process of developing a website that fosters community growth or producing resources that improve residents' practice of community life could provide the members of the inquiry groups with tremendous possibilities to discover what Southton truly needs to flourish. In addition, while it seemed clear that participants were learning from the project, the framework lacked an assessment strategy that would reveal what types of learning were occurring. As a result, future efforts need to address this limitation by developing more detailed processes to determine the nature of the social learning taking place and evaluate how this social learning can translate into real benefits for the community.

Recommendations for Practice

Although the pilot study was too small and limited to propose definitive policy interventions, the inquiry groups' discussion suggests a need for a broad community relations strategy focused on two areas. The first area, suggested by Group A, lies in addressing basic information deficits within the community regarding local events and issues and promoting community-level conversations about local concerns, such as business development, access to food and other necessities, quality of life, and, of course, the opioid epidemic. These conversations can occur in a variety of formats, whether they are technically mediated through a website or social media platform or through a series of community forums that bring residents to talk and debate together. Mark Button and David Michael Ryle (2005) argue that deliberative forums can take a variety of forms, some adversarial but others focused on increasing learning and understanding. Forums can be sponsored by community associations, nonprofits, or government agencies, and participants can be solicited through a general invitation to the community or more targeted efforts to ensure that the participants are representative of the community's diversity. For the purposes of the opioid epidemic, issues forums—non-adversarial, informal, issues-based, exploratory discussions driven by ordinary people under the guidance of facilitators trained to coach and probe the conversation forward (see Melville, Willingham, and Dedrick 2005)—seem particularly important.

Whatever form these conversations take, however, the PCI framework emphasizes that they need to be rooted within the Southton community, run by community members, and focused on sharing and conversation instead of top-down information delivery. As Lyn Carson and Janette Hartz-Karp (2005) observe, effective forums must have the ability to influence the policy conversation, include a diversity of perspectives and values, and offer participants the freedom and respect to establish a working consensus on important issues. Such an approach would also attend to what Pat Gehrke (2018) and Lerner and Gehrke (2018) call the community's *communication ecology*, which would reflect the multiple and conflicting interests in play, Southton's unique social context and values, and the various pressures that the community is experiencing. Gehrke argues that forum designers cannot presume that they know or understand the context and the knowledge, beliefs, and needs of the participants. Each forum needs to attend to the specific concerns of the space and place where it occurs. "Recipes, stock blueprints, and even previously successful models can all have a place in the preparation of effective communication and public engagement, but they must always be adapted to the communication situation at hand," he writes (2018, 67). "The ingredients available are different in every communication situation; blueprints must be modified to fit the terrain and space available." Beginning the conversation in this way, he continues, not only makes for a more amicable discussion but also allows policy makers to realize something that can be easily forgotten in a society defined by technocratic and meritocratic expertise: Local residents have tremendous wisdom to share that enables them to be not only partners in the community's future, but also its leaders capable of taking action in their own right.

The second area of need, emphasized by Group B, involves deeper work in helping members of the community develop the capacity necessary to build the community they want to see. Addressing this complex problem requires a much more extensive process of inquiry and learning that can reach beyond the efforts of a single group and, if successful, would address the three major limitations of the current study. Simply put, the social learning that Group B desires requires a larger, more diverse group who can talk, work, and learn together over an extended period. Without this process, any effort to develop and offer resources would only further strengthen the dark side of social capital (Putnam 2000) and, in turn, increase frustration and division within the community.

This broad-based effort first requires finding ways of including marginalized groups—not only racial, ethnic, and sexual minorities but also, most especially in this case, people in recovery—into the process. Here, Gregory C. Ellison II's (2017) Fearless Dialogues Project, which was developed to foster constructive conversations among religious congregations on race and racism, may offer a particularly promising addition to PCI. When communities face crises, Ellison argues, all too often the task of responding falls to the same group of leaders whose rivalries frustrate conversation and force them back to their familiar positions. Drawing together facilitated conversation and numerous forms of artistic expression around painful topics, fearless dialogues serve as what Ellison calls a form of quiet resistance that challenges people to see, hear, and change themselves and their communities in new ways. "When unlikely partners come to see individuals around them as innately gifted human beings, then they can hear the stories of people from seemingly different backgrounds as valuable," he writes. "With the capacity to see gifts and hear wisdom within unfamiliar stories, the pump is primed for unlikely partners to pursue change" (12). Fearless dialogues seem particularly important in helping diverse groups in divided communities establish an affirmative intent and surface the social goods that are key to a successful PCI initiative. What is more, the faith-based foundation of fearless dialogues may speak well to the strong network of churches within the Southton community and the social goods both groups wanted to advance.

Keeping such a large, diverse group together over an extended period, however, is impossible. As a result, these larger-scale events need to be combined with smaller groups focused on developing practices and testing them through actions. Zaid Hassan's (2014) model of social labs could be helpful. Social labs assemble a diverse team of activists, makers, community leaders, and others who come from a variety of different perspectives and disciplines to address systemic problems through inquiry and experimentation. While Hassan recognizes that a single social lab working alone cannot address complex challenges, what he calls *ecologies* of social labs experimenting in communication with each other—similar to networks of laboratories in the natural and applied sciences—might be able to make progress in addressing these issues. Hassan's model suggests that a community like Southton requires multiple PCI inquiry groups inquiring into the community, acknowledging goods, and proposing practices and actions that promote lasting change.

Such an effort requires extensive coordination to help PCI initiatives realize the change they desire to create. Mary Emery, Ken Hubbell, and Becky Miles-Polka's (2011) work on what they call community coaching may be important in facilitating this process. Unlike consulting models focusing on the consultant's expertise at the expense of what may be truly appropriate or necessary in a given situation, coaching embraces what Emery and her co-authors call *co-learning*, which they see as essential at the community level, where no single expert can see the entire system. Community coaching, they continue, helps community members learn new ways of communicating and engaging one another so that they can grow to meet the problems they face:

> At a very basic level, successful community coaching moves people from a needs-based approach to an asset or strength-based approach to community work. Coaching for communities means offering an empathetic ear, finding the coachable moments and engaging in joint learning. Coaches do not provide the answers; they support capacity building by helping community members learn from one another and from their own experiences in order to find their own solutions.
>
> (2011, 9)

Community coaching, Emery and her co-authors write, is about building relationships between people grounded in trust and respect. When
done well, it can help complex groups clarify their interests and goals,
discover new possibilities, analyze and assess their situation and capacity to respond to it, pursue more transformational work, improve
decision-making and organizational structures, improve resilience in
response to setbacks and changes, and highlight and affirm fundamental values.

Within Emery and her colleagues' (2011) model, community coaching has three levels. The first, which they call *itinerary and resources*,
focuses on identifying strengths and suggesting a way forward. The
second, which they name *routes, strategies, values*, identifies different
opportunities and scenarios that can help the community overcome
obstacles. The third, *transformation, new destinations, and possibilities*, opens the possibility of more radical types of change in the
community's sense of mission, self-understanding, and institutional
environment. The three phases of this model echo the three components of PCI in compelling ways: Engaging a community with an
appreciative intent surfaces social goods and resources and shapes
the effort's itinerary; proposing and testing practices can be essential for strategizing and route-finding; and designing actions fosters
the learning necessary to help a community find its new destination.
In this sense, PCI is not simply a model for participatory research
but also becomes a model of community coaching in its own right,
helping communities discover possibilities in a time of extraordinary
challenge and change.

References

Button, Mark, and David Michael Ryle. 2005. "What Can We Learn from
the Practice of Deliberative Democracy?" In *The Deliberative Democracy
Handbook*, edited by John Gastil and Peter Levine, 20–33. San Francisco,
CA: Jossey-Bass.

Carson, Lyn, and Janette Hartz-Karp. 2005. "Adapting and Combining
Deliberative Designs: Juries, Polls, and Forums." In *The Deliberative De-
mocracy Handbook*, edited by John Gastil and Peter Levine, 120–38. San
Francisco, CA: Jossey-Bass.

Ellison, Gregory C., II. 2017. *Fearless Dialogues: A New Movement for Justice.*
Louisville, KY: Westminster John Knox Press.

Emery, Mary, Ken Hubbell, and Becky Miles-Polka. 2011. *A Field Guide to
Community Coaching.* Battle Creek, MI: W. K. Kellogg Foundation.

Gehrke, Pat J. 2018. *Nano-Publics: Communicating Nanotechnology Applications, Risks, and Regulations.* New York: Springer International Publishing.

Hassan, Zaid. 2014. *The Social Labs Revolution: A New Approach to Solving Our Most Complex Challenges.* San Francisco, CA: Berrett-Koehler Publishers.

Kurtz, Cynthia F. 2014. *Working with Stories in Your Community or Organization: Participatory Narrative Inquiry.* 3rd ed. Northville, NY: Kurtz-Fernhout Publishing.

Lerner, Adam S., and Pat J. Gehrke. 2018. *Organic Public Engagement: How Ecological Thinking Transforms Public Engagement with Science.* New York: Palgrave.

Melville, Keith, Taylor L. Willingham, and John R. Dedrick. 2005. "National Issues Forums: A Network of Communities Promoting Public Deliberation." In *The Deliberative Democracy Handbook*, edited by John Gastil and Peter Levine, 37–58. San Francisco, CA: Jossey-Bass.

Putnam, Robert. 2000. *Bowling Alone: The Collapse and Revival of American Community.* New York: Simon & Schuster.

Conclusion

Becoming the Great Community

The movement John Dewey (1991) hoped to see within American life toward the Great Community was never fulfilled, and the work of Robert Bellah and his colleagues (1985, 1991) decades later underscores the imaginative and structural obstacles to Dewey's vision that have only become worse with time. Today, Americans struggle with even the most basic tasks of social cooperation, as demonstrated by the confusion and conflict over how to best respond to COVID-19, police violence and racial inequality, the growing gap between rich and poor, the rise of deaths of despair, and global climate change and the prospect of environmental collapse, to name a few. But as Bellah and his co-authors argued, the difficulties we face today in framing the public conversations we need are not simply problems of information transmission. Moving from transaction to communication has always been an ethical issue that depends on our ability to attend to others, be present to others, and care for the common spaces that bring us together—a capacity this study has defined as communal literacy.

If communal literacy is in decline, how do we strengthen it? The framework of Participatory Community Inquiry (PCI), which is appreciative in intent, practice-driven, and action-oriented, offers both scholars of communication ethics and community organizers a potentially useful system-level intervention that can help community members deepen their ability to think about and rebuild the social connections that are essential for meaningful lives together. The project in Southton suggests that the framework can generate productive conversations about what matters most and lead to practices and action steps that can yield important benefits within a community. Although the project focused on the opioid epidemic in one particularly afflicted area, PCI may be fruitful for helping communities build the ethical capacity to engage in the complex conversations our moment demands. To be sure, this framework needs additional adjustment and

DOI: 10.4324/9781003243663-8

refinement. But if these refinements can be made, this study suggests that PCI can have important implications not only for community life and relations but also for organizational development and leadership, as institutions of all types wrestle with similar problems, from diversity and inclusion to workplace harassment and bullying to community relations in an increasingly complex world.

The question, of course, is when and how we will be able to have these conversations. At the time of this writing, Americans are emerging from the stresses of a pandemic to find a country incorrigibly divided along lines of race, class, and political ideology. As of the time of this writing in fall 2021, we have no idea when a group of strangers of any size will be comfortable sitting next to each other close enough to share what matters most to them. Even though Americans may soon be able to leave their cloth masks behind, their faces and voices remain muffled and distorted by invisible masks woven by animosity and resentment. Indeed, the isolation of social distancing and the inability to see the face of the Other—both figuratively and literally—now appear to have diminished communal literacy all the more. Yet, these concerns should deepen our resolve. What better time would there be for Americans to rediscover the challenges and joys of living and talking together? Our willingness to answer this question will determine the future of the country we share.

References

Bellah, Robert N., Richard Madsen, William M. Sullivan, Ann Swidler, and Steven M. Tipton. 1985. *Habits of the Heart: Individualism and Commitment in American Life*. Berkeley: University of California Press.

———. 1991. *The Good Society*. New York: Vintage.

Dewey, John. 1991. *The Public and Its Problems*. Athens, OH: Swallow Press.

Index

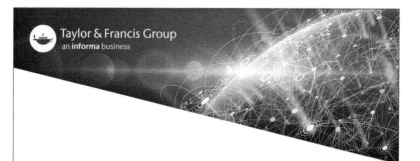